TOUCHED BY ANGELS

IS BLESSED BY CRITICAL PRAISE ...

"Impossible to put down....Engrossing and inspiring. The true stories are compelling and well told, and demonstrate the astounding ways angels intervene in our lives....A meaty book long on substance."

—Rosemary Guiley, *Fate*

"Contains true-life accounts that are nothing short of miraculous."
—*Lincoln Journal & Star* (NE)

"A well-informed mix of traditional lore, Eileen's own earnest quest for the truth, and a number of other people's personal accounts. It offers useful guidelines to help readers determine whether or not they've encountered angels."

—Alma Daniel, author of *Ask Your Angels*

"Every page of TOUCHED BY ANGELS is warm and delicious reading....Eileen's solid nine-point checklist offers real help to those wishing to test spiritual encounters, and make sure they are heaven-sent."

—Joan Wester Anderson, author of *Where Angels Walk: True Stories of Heavenly Visitors*

"Fascinating glimpses of something miraculous, seemingly divine intervention into people's lives."

—*Library Journal*

"An uplifting collection of traditional lore and eyewitness accounts...heartening evidence that heavenly beings are at work."
—*The Literary Guild* magazine

Touched by Angels

Eileen Elias Freeman

WARNER BOOKS

A Time Warner Company

Copyright © 1993 by Eileen Elias Freeman
All rights reserved.

Warner Books, Inc., 1271 Avenue of the Americas, New York, NY 10020

 A Time Warner Company

Printed in the United States of America
First Trade Printing: September 1994
10 9 8 7 6

Originally published in hardcover by Warner Books, Inc.

Library of Congress Cataloging-in-Publication Data
Freeman, Eileen E.
    Touched by angels / Eileen Elias Freeman.
      p. cm.
    ISBN 0-446-67033-2
    1. Angels. 2. Guardian angels. I. Title
    BL477.F74 1993
    291.2'15—dc20   93-10231
                                    CIP

Book design by Giorgetta Bell McRee
Cover design by Paul Gamarello
Cover art: "Angel of The Annunciation" by Fra Angelico,
*   courtesy of Superstock*

To my parents, Helen and Alex Freeman,
who always said I'd be a WRITER.

Contents

Contents

Contents

Are they not all ministering spirits, sent to serve those who are to inherit salvation?

—Letter to the Hebrews 1:14

Foreword

To say that 1992 was a watershed year for general awareness of angels and their work in the world today may sound dramatic, but I believe it's true. For the past two hundred years or so, the angels of God have been increasingly visible in their deeds and actions as powerful forces of good for the human race. In the past fifty years, they have stepped up their work in our midst; and in the past decade our awareness of angelic activity has increased beyond anything I believe this world has ever seen. Not only are people by the thousands reporting that their lives have been recently touched by angels, but many others have gained the courage to speak of life-transforming events dating back decades earlier, when an angelic encounter changed the course of their destiny.

In 1992, led, as I believe, by my own guardian angel, whom I call Enniss, I started The AngelWatch Network™, a clearinghouse for all information about angels and what they are doing in today's world. I began a bimonthly magazine to keep interested individuals—angelwatchers, as I call them—up to date about angels in the news and in people's lives, and I sought out publicity in the media, to focus attention on the presence and work of angels in our midst.

The angels saw to it that I was successful. Letters and cards poured in by the hundreds, begging for information and sharing their own. Some days my phone rang off the hook with angelwatchers. I answered the inquiries as well as time and budget allowed. And every time I thought there was no more time, the angels would find it for me. Whenever the money for more printing got low, a flood of new subscriptions or speaking engagements would right the balance. When a story in the media had run its course, another reporter would call out of the blue for another story, and more interest would be generated. The angels even managed to direct mail marked "The Angel Lady of Mt. Side NY" to my correct P.O. Box 1362 in Mountainside, New Jersey. The signs of their activity were obvious. Even writers who called for interviews said that for the first time in their careers, everyone they needed to interview was available and willing the first time around, and that their stories practically wrote themselves.

Clearly, the ancient servants of God and humanity have a mission, a God-given plan to help us grow in wisdom and love, not just so that we will survive as a race, but so we will be able to grow into what we were always intended to be—perfected beings capable of incredible energies and immense, transforming love.

Touched by Angels is about that angelic mission and about some of the people who have become a part of it in an unusual way, men and women linked together by a common thread—an angelic encounter that changed their lives forever. It presents some very special true stories of people who have actually encountered angels and been touched by their message and whose lives were altered forever as a result. And it describes in some detail how these encounters happen, and how we can tell them apart from our own personal desire for such an encounter or our wishful thinking and imagination.

The people whose stories are told in this book are real. In most cases they have decided to use their real names and cities; in one (Robin Diettrick) I was asked to use a pseudonym, and I agreed, because her story was so inspirational. She was concerned that identifying her might subject her family (her husband is still in the military) to publicity that they didn't want, with the possibility of unforeseen consequences. (I understood this quite well—after I made a television appearance on *The Jerry Springer Show* in December of 1992, the company for which I had worked fired me. I had held a very visible position in the company, and it viewed my public interest in and discussion of angels as too uncorporate [read "just plain weird"] to be tolerated.)

If you have been touched by an angel, I would be especially pleased to hear from you. By sharing the wonderful evidences in our lives of God's love for us, we help make this world a more beautiful, more love-filled place for us—and our angels—to live.

Eileen Elias Freeman
The AngelWatch Network
P.O. Box 1362
Mountainside, New Jersey
07092

Acknowledgments

Acknowledgment is such a silly word—as though I could just "acknowledge" grace from heaven, the love and support of my family and friends, the special help of my own angels, who are glad this book is finally written, and of my parents, Helen and Alex Freeman, who see me now with the eyes of God.

But I need to thank a number of beings for their help and support, and I guess acknowledgment will have to do—at least in this world.

On the human side: my sister-cousin Carol who not only gave me moral support but personally licked hundreds of stamps to mail out *AngelWatch* while I worked on the book; my Uncle Tom, who kept calling for progress reports; Marilynn Webber, friend and angelwatcher *extraordinaire* from California, who listened patiently while I bounced all kinds of ideas off her ears; Joan Wester

Acknowledgments

Anderson, friend and author of *Where Angels Walk*, who prayed with me on the phone and offered wise advice in the Spirit; my editor Joann Davis, whose enthusiasm has been a real delight; and all those in The AngelWatch Network, who have supported me with their prayers and letters.

Most especially, I want to thank the beautiful, generous people who shared their stories with me so that this book could be written. As I taped their interviews, sometimes we would find ourselves in tears, so strong were the events in their minds and hearts. I have no doubts that they have all been deeply touched by angels. I know I was touched just by being able to share their stories.

On the angelic side: To you, Enniss, my dear guardian, and to all who have assisted you, I offer public thanks for your faithful and loving service and guidance all my life. To God be the glory, but to you my deepest gratitude, and I pray that God will bless you, in whatever way angels can be blessed, for all you have done to bring me closer to the Source of all Life. I love you.

Touched by
Angels

Chapter One
Touched by Angels

I will give thanks to you, O Lord, with all my heart; in the presence of the angels I will sing your praise.   —Psalm 138:1

Everything I've ever said, written, collected, sung, appreciated, or done in regard to angels stems from one single event in my life—the first time I saw my own guardian angel, when I was five years old, and was touched—and changed—forever. That one event changed my life more than anything except the day I came to accept as an adult the belief that Jesus is indeed the true Lord of the Universe, and my Lord. In fact, I have always firmly believed that if my angel had not come to me when he did, I might never have lived to grow up to become an adult. I would have succumbed to the fears that dominated my life and given up. I would never have lived to experience the guiding presence of my angels in my life today.

* * *

It is said that our basic personalities are largely set by the time we are three or four. I know that by the time I was five, I was already a fearful child. I was afraid of the dark, afraid of the television set, the phone, most foods, and being separated from my parents, even for a moment. Mother couldn't even get out the vacuum cleaner without first sending me next door to my grandmother's, because the sound of the old Electrolux terrified me. I was an only, lonely child with two loving older parents who assumed I'd grow out of it. But I didn't.

I almost couldn't go to kindergarten, because the separation anxiety was terrifying. I can still remember my first day vividly. I was so excited I was sick to my stomach. Mother walked me to school—all two blocks—along with the other children and mothers and came into the classroom with me to introduce me to my teacher. Then, with a smile and a kiss, she left—and I panicked. I had never been in a classroom before, and I sat down on a chair and started to cry, and I cried, and cried, and cried. My teacher, who was an older woman and very kind, finally got me distracted, but I was so sick that I spent most of that first morning in the bathroom. It took almost a month before I could get through a day in kindergarten without tears and fears.

But even more than the terrors of fingerpaints and blocks, bedtime was the worst. I would close my eyes against the monsters and burglars I knew were out to get me and try to sleep. And when I could take the fear no more, I would go back downstairs crying. Mother would bring me back up to my bed and sit with me awhile; then she would return to the living room and the nighttime ritual of fear would continue. My fears were set against the backdrop of the Korean War, with radio accounts of torture and death, and I turned the atrocities into more nocturnal phantoms. A morbid, neurotic child? I certainly was.

Most of all, I was terrified by the thought of death. I don't know why a five-year-old should have considered such things more than her baby doll and her beloved set of Lionel trains, but I did. I went through a period when I was obsessed by death. Most children at five ask questions like "Why is the sky blue?" I asked, "Why do people die?" In fact, the thought was so frightening that my mother never did let me go to the movies to see *Bambi*, nor would she let me read the story—she knew that the little story would devastate me. When my kindergarten teacher was tragically killed in an auto accident near the end of my first year in school, I felt as if my world were starting to unravel. A familiar beacon of light and safety had been extinguished forever. Mother explained that my teacher had "gone to sleep," and that I would soon like my new teacher just as much. I quickly added "autophobia" to my list of fear. Taking me anywhere in the car became a difficult proposition, and for a while Mother would try to keep me distracted when my father left for work so I wouldn't see him leave in the car.

Then my turtle died. I found it soft and limp in the water. Mother explained that it had gone to sleep and we buried it in the backyard. I used to follow my Uncle Mike around the garden when he planted seeds. I knew what lived underground and what fate awaited the late Mr. Turtle.

And then my grandmother died. She was the only

grandparent I ever knew, and she represented to me the summit of wisdom.

Of course my parents never took me to the funeral home or the service or the grave. That wasn't done in the fifties. Mother told me that Grandma, like my teacher and my turtle, had just gone to sleep and wouldn't be coming back from the hospital anymore.

I thought about my turtle—and panicked. I thought about that beloved woman turning into food for worms, all because she had made the mistake of going to sleep one night. And, with the unmistakable logic of a child, I knew that I would be the next to go—just like the kids' gruesome song "The Worms Crawl In . . . "

The night after the funeral I refused to go to bed point-blank. My parents were sympathetic and let me stay up awhile longer, but soon even they insisted. I was terrified. I decided I would never sleep; I remember thinking something about dead people staying in their graves for three days and nights and then rising again, and wondering how Grandma was going to get out. I screamed and cried and became almost hysterical until my parents were quite upset. My father even suggested a small glass of his black-berry brandy—for purely medicinal purposes.

I finally fell asleep, more from exhaustion and the cordial than anything, but the next night it was the same thing all over. The only thing I remember about that night was that I was afraid of my train set, a large Lionel set that my father and I (mostly him, of course) had put together. It took up nearly a third of my bedroom. Mother was cross with me, but she had to cover it finally with a bed sheet.

I had a dread certainty that on the third night

Grandma would come and, because she had always loved me so much, would take me with her—somewhere. My ideas of heaven were very hazy, but I knew I didn't want to go there, at least not then. I had this awful dread that I, too, like all humanity, would have to spend three days and nights underground with the worms.

The third day after the funeral was a Saturday. For some reason I felt it was "safe" to sleep during the day, so I took a long, long nap. Mother complained that I would never sleep that night—and that was fine with me. If I could just stay awake all night, I would be safe forever.

I went to bed, nervous and determined, with a flashlight, purloined from the kitchen, and a Bobbsey Twins book (Grandma had taught me to read when I was three). I read under the covers as long as I could, until Mother came by and saw the light. Then I sat up in bed, cuddling my rag doll, whom I called Gretchen, with my back against the cold plaster wall behind me, trying not to let my fears overwhelm me. But it was no use. I remember being cold in a way I had never experienced before; even the air in the room seemed more like a dank, cold miasma, ghastly and awful. If you have ever been inside a meat locker, rank with the smell of death and of stale, bloody ice, you know what I mean.

I guess it must have been about ten o'clock when my angel came. I know it was not late. I know my parents were still up, because when I finally called them I heard Mother's step on the creaky stairs. The room was dark, except for the small night-light on the hall table, and the dim light coming in through the window over my radiator. From where I sat I could see out to the second-floor landing. To this day I can remember the wallpaper—off-white with sprays of climbing green ivy on trellises. In fact, the pattern has reemerged in recent years for lawn furniture and picnic-ware, and the mere sight of such items can bring back the whole experience to me.

I was staring across the room, where my doll's crib was, trying not to panic, when I noticed a kind of silvery mist beginning to obscure the sight of the crib. I refocused my eyes nearer and I saw that the silvery light was glowing softly at the foot of my bed. I wish I could describe the light, but I've never been really successful—it was too unearthly. It was soft like pewter, but it glowed from within. If a diamond were made of silver . . .

And as I watched this beautiful light, too fascinated to be afraid of the most unusual experience of my young life, a figure began to emerge out of the cloud.

Like the cloud, the figure was bathed in this incredible light, and I felt as though the light were reaching out to me, too. The being that appeared was rather tall and quite strong of physique, although I think my impression was more a mental one than a physical one. He—I knew the being was masculine—had very long and fine hair that seemed to flow and blow around him. His face was somewhat angular rather than smooth or rounded, and utterly serene. I never saw any wings, and the being's body seemed lost in the mist. In retrospect, I think that the angel only assumed as much of a humanlike appearance as he felt was necessary to communicate with me.

But what I remember most clearly—in fact, I can still see just by closing my eyes and recalling—were his eyes. They were very large and dark (although not abnormally so) and full of compassion for me and my fears. If you ask me, "What does compassion look like?" I would be hard-pressed to reply. But in those eyes I saw deep pity and compassion.

I remember sitting up straight in bed, away from the supporting wall, mesmerized by the apparition.

"Do not be afraid, Eileen," the figure said in a voice like pure crystal. "Your grandmother is not in a cold and dark grave. She is happy in heaven with God and her loved ones."

The being's words to me were like warm water—they melted the ice that had taken possession of my body and soul. My hands grew warm. The air, which had seemed frosty, now was like honey.

Who are you? I asked him silently.

"I am your guardian angel," he replied simply, in a practical sort of voice. "Always remember, there is nothing to be afraid of."

And then, before I could ask or say anything more, the angel began to fade back into the mist; then the silvery mist became transparent, and I could see my doll's crib once again.

At first I just sat there, not really knowing or understanding what had happened. All I could sense was that I was no longer afraid. It wasn't a feeling that the angel had chased away a monster; it was an understanding that the monster was even less substantial than the angel's mist. The angel had subtly changed something inside of me.

I looked over at my Lionel set, shrouded in a white sheet, and I was no longer afraid of it. It did not hide tiny monsters that would wake in the night to tie me up with little ropes and keep me prisoner, as Mother had once read me in a child's version of *Gulliver*.

I looked up at my windows, through which I had feared nightly monsters might come, and all I saw was the light from the back porch shining dimly through the curtains.

I thought about Grandma—and I knew, absolutely knew that my nighttime visitor had been right. She was not coming to get me. She was not moldering in her coffin. She had been freed from earth entirely and had gone to heaven to be with God and my grandfather and her two sons who had all died of influenza back in 1919 during the great pandemic.

When I had sorted out what I could, I called for Mother, who came running. I told her what had happened.

"What a lovely dream you've had, dear," she said, preoccupied with her own grieving for my grandmother and giving me a kiss. And then she returned downstairs to comfort my father, whose grief at losing his mother was profound. (The next day, prompted by Mother, he went to Canada to go fishing. When he returned a week later, he said he felt better, but he didn't bring home any fish.)

After Mother went downstairs, I realized that she did not believe me, and I was disappointed, but I think I understood that it was all right, even then. Truth to tell, my family was not especially religious, although we believed in God and my parents even sent me to a nearby Sunday School. Angels to my parents were creatures out of mythology that one associated with Christmas legends.

But I knew then, as I know now, that it was no dream.

I had been wide awake in the most exquisite terror of my life, and then, minutes later, I was warm and unafraid. I took one more look around the room, slipped down in the bed, breathed a sigh of relief, and went right to sleep.

When I woke the next day, it was late in the morning. Mother heard me stirring and came up to talk to me and to tell me that Daddy had gone fishing for a while. "I didn't dream about the angel, Mommy," I said.

She smiled.

I have often regretted that I never asked her to what she attributed the changes in me after that night. For when the phone rang, I was not afraid of it anymore. When she got out the vacuum cleaner, I stayed in the kitchen eating breakfast. I never even thought about being afraid. When we went to the store for groceries, I didn't feel the need to hold her hand tightly and cling to her. The angel had subtly changed more than my perception of death—he had altered my whole fearful approach to life.

In fact, that's how I know that my angelic encounter was real, and not a fantasy born of childhood desperation—because all of my fears disappeared in an instant when the angel told me not to be afraid, and they never came back. And since that day, I have never been afraid of death; to me it is simply an event in our lives, after which we move on to the joy that awaits the children of God. And I know it is real because, after nearly forty years, I have never been able to tell the story to anyone without crying.

I have never seen my angel again in that form. The night after my encounter, I stayed up for a long time, hoping that the wonderful, healing light and the being

9

who came to me would come again, but I was disappointed. I have never seen my guardian angel again in such magnificence. I have asked, but he has always said, "You don't need to see me in glory anymore."

Over the years I shared my encounter rarely, only with family members. To me it was a precious and dearly treasured moment, not to be talked about in the same way as one talked about homework, or playground gossip, or the like. As I got older and began to meditate on the significance of it, it seemed to me that it was too precious even to share with family. It was sacred, holy, and meant for me alone. It was solace when life became sad. It was encouragement at dark moments. It was joyful affirmation whenever I felt the light and love of God filling my life. It was a constant reminder of God's love for me.

As I began to set The AngelWatch Network in place, I found that people would ask me if I had had an angelic encounter. At first, I would just smile and nod. If asked to share it, I would shake my head and say, "It's just too personal." But in the summer of 1992, I attended a weekend workshop on angels given by Sophy Burnham, whose books on angels are well known. I felt myself being asked again and again to share my encounter, generally over the dinner table or while engaging in light conversation outside of the workshop sessions. Again I declined to share. It just didn't seem right to tell the whole story while stuffing my mouth with pickled beets, and I never told an abbreviated form of the story—I either told the whole thing or I didn't tell it at all.

On Sunday, however, during the workshop, I felt my guardian angel speak to me deep in my heart. I had been meditating and praying about whether I should share. It's hard on me, because whenever I do, I relive the entire encounter, and I find myself crying and emotionally drained afterward. But while I was asking my angel if I should share, I felt him say yes quite clearly. So, when the opportune moment came, I took a deep breath, and asked for the microphone.

I was crying long before I finished my story, and many in the group of nearly one hundred were crying with me. One man even said afterward that, for him, it was the most important part of the whole workshop. And in further meditation, my angel told me that from now on, I was to tell the story to anyone who asked, and that I was not to worry about where or when the story would be heard. "God will use your story to lead people closer to the Light," he said. And I have seen that when I pay close attention to the story, God does grace the hearts of those who hear it. It is a joyful and a humbling thing.

People often ask me how I can remember so many things about that time. "Aren't you reading back into it all your adult thoughts?" they ask. The more I think about it, the more the answer to that question is no. As I look back on forty years of thinking about the story and telling it, the astonishing thing to me is that the story hasn't changed a bit. I haven't created a choir of angels in the background or a long dialogue between the angel and myself. The story today is as it was in 1952.

Of course some things have changed. In 1952 I wasn't a writer with a gift for wordsmithery and the ability to choose the very best words to describe my encounter. At five, I didn't know about pearl and pewter and silver as colors to describe the radiance of the angel. I could only say, "It was like white, but it wasn't."

* * *

As I have become more involved with the work of the angels, I have met many people who have seen their angels when they were children. What strikes me is the incredible amount of detail they remember. So I don't think my recollection of the event is all that extraordinary.

Apart from freeing me from the fear of death, my angel also planted seeds inside me that would grow into a great hunger to know more about God and the dimension we call heaven or the Kingdom. I started keeping diaries of meditations when I was eleven, in which I would write thoughts that came to me about God and the angels. I read through them now and I don't see anything profound, but it's clear that my angel had awakened in me a longing to know God and to be part of that glorious hymn of creation that is sung by all of God's children. I surprised my parents immensely by telling them that I thought I belonged in the Roman Catholic Church, and would they mind if I started to go there instead of the Episcopalian church I had attended. They were not receptive at first, but after five years of my persevering, they finally consented to my becoming a Catholic.

I'm convinced that it was God's plan for me to do so, for in that milieu my belief in the immanent help of the servants of God grew rapidly. The Catholic tradition has always accepted supernatural intervention as a normal part of life, in fact, essential to life, and such supernatural help included angels. I had no doubts as I went to school, and then to college, that my angel was with me to guide me.

I have to confess, though, that until I entered college

as a comparative religion major, I never even imagined the scope of angelic work and activity in the history of the world. Studying the different religious systems— Western, Eastern—I began to see just how universal the angels of God are. Virtually every religious system I studied contained beings whose mission and activities were comparable to that of the angels I knew. Sometimes they were called kami or peri, or fravashi. Sometimes they were seen as demigods or sons and daughters of the gods. But in most respects, they were messengers, guardians, protectors.

The Hand on My Shoulder

I had never thought of my guardian angel as a protector until one day late in my senior year—1970. While I was at Barnard, I had been as active religiously and politically as I could. In trying to come close to the Light that is God, I saw how blessed I was, and, while always trying to live more fully in the light, I felt the need to do what I could to make life better for others. I was part of a small group that met together to celebrate the Eucharist in people's homes and to plan activities like working in the food bank or protesting injustice with social action groups across Morningside Park in Harlem.

One day I walked up Broadway to 121st Street, where a good friend of mine in the group lived. We had planned to meet to discuss a home Mass that was to take place the next week. It was a very ordinary day. I don't even remember what the weather was like.

On my right, I passed the gates of Columbia, Earle Hall (the religious activities building), classrooms, Teacher's College; on my left, across the busy Broadway street, was Barnard, my alma mater.

I turned right onto 121st Street. Victor's apartment was in a commonplace apartment building halfway up the block. Across from it was Corpus Christi Church, a beautiful church, all white and Georgian, sandwiched in between other buildings, but nonetheless charming.

I approached Victor's apartment building and set my right foot on the first step.

Suddenly, I felt a strong hand on my left shoulder that effectively brought me to a dead stop. I whirled around, concerned that someone who meant me no good might be there. (I had been mugged once in my sophomore year, and although I was not harmed, it was still a spooky experience.)

No one was there.

Surprised, I looked around, as though I expected to see somebody disappearing around a corner. But the street was virtually empty. No one was near enough to have touched me.

As silly as it seems to me today, I even looked up into the sky, wondering if maybe a bird . . .

After a minute, I turned back to the apartment steps and again put my right foot on the first step.

This time the hand on my shoulder not only brought me to a full stop, but almost jerked me backward. Once more I whirled around, but the street was just as empty as before.

It was then that I heard my guardian angel's voice, as

clear as a bell ringing through a cold, crisp night: "It would not be wise for you to go in there just now."

I recognized that voice at once, although I had not heard it for sixteen years, and my heart leaped with joy. I looked around anxiously, hoping that this was the moment when I would see him again, as an adult, and give him the thanks I had always tried to convey, but face-to-face.

But he was not there.

I looked up at the apartment building. It seemed so ordinary; yet my guardian angel had just told me not to go in. Or had he? His words were, "It would not be wise . . ." Should I or shouldn't I? After all, I was supposed to meet Victor and the reason was fairly important. I couldn't decide.

I looked at my watch and realized that I still had a little time before we were supposed to meet. Just then the church bells of Notre Dame, another parish church a few blocks away, sounded the quarter hour. *I know,* I thought to myself, *I'll go into Corpus Christi and make a little "visit"*—as private Catholic devotions were called.

I went across the small residential street and into the church. I genuflected and knelt down in a pew for a short prayer; then I sat back and began to think about what had just happened.

My angel had just stopped me from visiting my friend and had told me it wouldn't be wise. Well, what was there about planning a Mass that wouldn't be wise? Was there something about Victor that wasn't wise? Was our little society not wise?

It's a personal fault that I often make mountains out

of molehills. My angel's words were simple and direct, but for at least fifteen minutes I tried to read a world of subtlety into them.

I was still trying to decide what I should do, when I began to hear the sirens. At first they were soft and distant, and I paid them no attention. After all, one expects to hear sirens in New York City. But as they became louder and louder and increased in number, the noise was too great to ignore. In fact, they sounded as though they were right outside the door.

Curious, I got up, made my reverence, and walked out into the vestibule.

I opened the door—and got a shock.

In front of Victor's apartment building were at least four police and emergency vehicles, sirens just winding down, lights flashing. Officers, guns drawn, were running inside. As I—automatically—ran across the street, a fire fighter politely stopped me, telling me it was an emergency and I must clear the area. I did so at once. In fact, I didn't stop running until I turned the corner and was back on Broadway again. More police cars were heading toward 121st Street as I reentered my dorm building.

I was shaken all afternoon by what had happened. But what *had* happened? I had no idea, and there was no answer at Victor's phone. Soon it was time for me to go to a four o'clock class in sociology of religion, and it wasn't until after the five o'clock Mass and dinner in the dorm that I got back to my room.

I really ought to try to get hold of Victor, I thought, picking up the phone and dialing. This time he answered.

I apologized for not meeting him as we had agreed. To tell the truth, I didn't know at that moment whether I would have told him about the warning my angel had given me.

"I didn't think you would have been able to get in," he answered at once. "You saw all the cop cars, well, there was a woman murdered in the elevator—stabbed to death by a drug dealer. It was awful. They came through and asked to search all our apartments. I think they got him, though."

He went on, but I wasn't listening. I felt my stomach thud with a queer sort of lurch, and I sat down hard on my bed. *My God!* I thought. If my angel hadn't warned me, I might have been the one who was killed.

I made some appropriate answer to Victor's comments and eventually got off the phone. I found I was shaking with shock, fear, relief—I couldn't separate out the strands. But then I heard in my mind the words my angel had said to me when I was a child, "There is nothing to be afraid of," and slowly I calmed down. Now I knew what he had meant when he had advised me not to go into the apartment building. I knelt down and gave thanks. I promised that I would always give thanks to God for the protection and care of my guardian angel, and that I would do what I could to spread the word that all of us have these wonderful guardians in our lives.

I never did talk about this encounter very much. Perhaps in a university atmosphere I had even less certainty than as a child of being believed. But I think the main reason was that I knew people would ask me, "But how did you know it was your guardian angel?" And at that time in my life, I just didn't want to share my childhood story.

After college I went on to graduate school at the University of Notre Dame, where I earned a master's and worked toward a doctorate in theology, with a concentration in the scriptures, liturgy, and the early Christian writers. I began to see more clearly the different ways that our angels have worked not only with us as individuals, but as groups, and I also began to write about them for academic and liturgical publications. And yet I still kept silence about my own experiences.

The Pilot Program

In September of 1979 my guardian angel and certain other angels who serve God with him began to teach me a number of things about the way their society is organized and the nature and abilities of angels. This series of intuitions went on, on virtually a daily basis, for nearly three years.

At the time these interior visions began, I was living in Glendale, Arizona, and working for a church music-publishing company. One evening, while I was sitting peacefully in my living room working on my stamp collection, I began to sense the presence of God in an unusual way for me. It began with a kind of sensory deprivation, in which my attention gradually focused inward. I no longer heard the stereo that was on in the background or saw the room around me. All the objects in front of me became two-dimensional, so to speak, and utterly colorless. I was drawn so deep inside my own heart, my own soul, that I lost all awareness of the external world.

And deep in my heart, I saw the shadow of God, so bright I could not look at it, and I felt that shadow filling me with light and peace. It seemed as though all of the conflicting thoughts and duties and attitudes we all must deal with daily had been evened out, smoothed away; and I was so utterly tranquil I have no words to describe it. For one moment, it seemed as though my body, mind, and soul were all agreed in perfect harmony, all focused on the Source of their being. It was a time of enormous joy, and wordlessly I gave thanks to God for giving me such an experience, such a foretaste of the harmony of heaven, for that is what I felt my experience to be. It is called in the mystical literature *infused contemplation*—a moment when God draws the unsuspecting soul deep into the mystery of divinity. It is Spirit-sent enlightenment, not humanly acquired knowledge, and it has nothing to do with whether one is an ordinary person or a saint, spiritually aware or totally unknowing.

For some time I just sat there in perfect peace, sunk deep inside my heart, where the light of God shines in each of us. And then I heard a voice coming from that center of my being. It said, "I am Enniss, servant of God, and your guardian by divine grace; and you are my ward in this world."

I knew the voice at once, even though it seemed to be coming from inside me. It was the voice that had reassured me as a child and as an adult, the voice of my guardian angel. And I knew the name was right, although I had never heard it before.

Then I heard other voices. It will sound strange, no doubt, if I say that, although the other voices all sounded the same, I knew they belonged to different beings.

"I am Asendar, who leads the Guardians of your race, and Enniss's superior."

"I am Kennisha, who serves the Most High as a protector of your race."

"I am Tallithia. I keep the record, that all heaven may see and wonder."

As I listened to these inner voices, I heard music, if one can call it that, so incredible that I have no words for it. It was as if the entire world was a bolt of cloth and each thread sang a different song that harmonized perfectly with all the others, and, at the points where thread crossed thread, a counterpoint of percussion moved the whole along, and the sound rippled and flowed through my being until I do believe I physically got up from my chair and began to dance all alone with uncounted beings in my living room. If this was music, it sang on the wavelengths of light, colors, and hues beyond human eyesight; I saw ultraviolet and infrared and spectra we have not yet named, gradations of color that healed, that created, that loved, caused, and were caused. I felt that if I could have filled a plate with those colors I could have been nourished by them for a hundred life spans. I wanted to follow the music, the color, the dance to the feet of the One who had created them. . . .

It was about two hours later that the inner vision slowly faded. Ordinary human sensation returned, and I became aware of my surroundings. I touched the arm of my chair; I could feel the nubby texture. Objects around me—typewriter, stamp stock books, album pages—were as they had been. The stereo radio was still playing—something by Anne Murray, as I recall. But for a while yet I was so disoriented I did not know what to make of these ordinary things. I felt as if I had been holding my breath for two hours. I stood up slowly and walked into the kitchen to get some water. Whatever journey my spirit had just returned from, my body was thirsty. I went to sleep soon after.

The next day I went to an early Mass. I tried to go to church most days; I have always been the sort who finds worship in common a helpful spiritual practice. Then I headed out to a desert park north of the city with my typewriter, a Bible, a gallon of water, and the intention of spending some time in prayer and meditation about the extraordinary event of the night before. And while there, surrounded by saguaro and cholla and jackrabbits, I began to meditate on the names that I had heard: Enniss, Kennisha, Asendar, Tallithia. It had never really been brought home to me before that a human might have more than one angel to guard and guide. (In Islam, for example, people are seen as having two—a guardian angel and the recording angel who takes note of the person's words and deeds.)

I prayed as sincerely and as humbly as I knew how, asking the Spirit to show me what all of this might mean, and how I should judge the vision. I knew that most human visions are just that; they proceed from our own intelligence and insight, and although they can be good and positive, they are not gifts from heaven. Was that what had happened to me? I wondered for a long time. I thought, *It was just your longing for God that caused it to happen. After all, you are a most ordinary person, Eileen, and as anyone who has ever cut you off on the highway or*

21

*fumbled too long with change in the check-out line knows,
you're so far from being* saintly *that your guardian must tear
his hair out in frustration ten times a day.*

But as I thought about the fruits of what I had experienced, I began to realize that there was no way I could
have, even unknowingly, counterfeited the light, the
color, the music, and, most of all, the sense of peace and
joy I had experienced in the depths of my soul. They were
all far beyond my ken. Only God could have showered my
spirit with such wonders.

It took me most of the morning to be perfectly sure in
my mind that my experience was not a delusion or a
figment of my own imagination. At that point the names,
which I had put aside for the time, came flooding back.
If the vision was real, I thought, then the names were
real, the angels were real.

I turned to Jesus in prayer and I asked him to open my
heart to whatever He might want to teach me through
his servants, the angels; and in prayer I named them:
Enniss, Asendar, Kennisha, Tallithia. Then I addressed
each of them, saying that I would try to listen to whatever
God might want to say. It was easy to address Enniss; I
could see the face he had turned toward me in my childhood days whenever I closed my eyes. I knew the name
Enniss was right. I do not believe, of course, that that is
the "real" name of my guardian, but I do believe he wants
me to call him by that name for now.

I did not expect to receive any overt response to my
sincere prayers, and I did not, but I nonetheless typed up
an account of that morning before getting back into the
car for the trip home.

Hoping that I would receive further enlightenment

about what the names might mean for me, I began spending at least two hours a day in solitary prayer and meditation, not trying to analyze, but just to be open to grace. And I found that at the oddest moments I would have flashes of what I believed and still do believe, were insights from God through Enniss about the dimension called heaven and the angelic beings who help us humans in our quest to live in the fullness of that dimension.

At first, I was unsure what to make of these thoughts. I wrote them down, of course; I developed a habit of staying in church for an hour or so after Mass just reading through them and asking God for enlightenment. Then one day, I decided to write a sort of spiritual journal, not a blow-by-blow account of each day, but an ongoing exploration of the spiritual realities I was thinking so much about. I had no idea that it would ever be read by anyone than myself, so I mixed in fantasy and speculation with the day's events, and I explored to the limits the insights that I was receiving on virtually a daily basis. I do not mean that God was thundering in my ear about the angels in a daily series of rapt contemplations. I mean that as I persevered in daily, homely, honest meditation, I often saw things about the angelic orders that I felt should be recorded.

These inner lights and insights continued for nearly three years. By that time I had returned to my family's home in New Jersey, where my father, who was dying of lung cancer, and my mother both required help. I kept my "journal" and my meditations regularly. By the time Enniss told me that the initial work was finished, it had become a four-volume, twelve-hundred-page work that I named *The Guardians of the Earth*. I divided it into four

23

volumes based on periods of unusually strong insights I had received: *The Pilot Program*, in which Enniss describes a new sort of relationship that is now beginning to develop between angels and humans; *The House of Healing*, which shows how we can work with the angels through the medium of God's grace to heal our lives of evil and darkness; *The Rituals of God*, which explores the ways heaven and earth are growing closer together as this present age winds down; and *The Percivale Riddle*, which envisions a world in which angels and humans cooperate in a new and stronger way than ever before to transform this world. The insights about angels are such as I received, explored, and tested, while many of the externals in the books are fantasy, fiction.

As I said, at no time did I ever consider publishing these volumes. At the core of my being I am an intensely private person, and the thought of exposing so much of my soul was impossible. But I continued to read and reread the volumes, and I even began the momentous task of converting them to a computer file in 1988, shortly after my mother had entered the fullness of the Kingdom.

About a year later, I came to the realization that my journals should be published, and that I had perhaps even been hindering the work of change and enlightenment by hanging back out of fear of having my innermost thoughts exposed. But the work of retyping twelve hundred pages was daunting, and my own schedule precluded such intensive effort. So I did what in some religious circles is called laying a fleece. It's a naive sort of thing: you set certain unusual conditions and if they are fulfilled, you take it as a sign from heaven. I put up a notice in a

Christian bookstore: I HAVE A 1200-PAGE MANUSCRIPT
ABOUT ANGELS THAT NEEDS TO BE REKEYED AS A COM-
PUTER WORD-PROCESSING FILE. THE GOOD NEWS: ANY KIND
OF PC FILE WILL DO, AND TIME IS NOT A FACTOR. THE BAD
NEWS: IT'S TYPED SINGLE-SPACED ON BOTH SIDES OF VERY
THIN PAPER WITH A SCRIPT TYPE-BALL, HALF OF IT IS
DIALOGUE (LOTS OF QUOTATION MARKS!) AND IT'S NOT
EDITED, SO IT'S FULL OF TYPOS. I CAN PAY A MAXIMUM OF
50 CENTS PER PAGE. The idea that any typist would take
on such a project for such a ridiculously low price made
it unlikely in my eyes that I would get any response, but
by the time I got home after posting the notice, there
was a message on my answering machine from a woman
who said she was interested in angels and would be glad
to type the whole thing at the price I had mentioned.

At that point, I knew that my guardian angel had been
right when he had said that God's plan was for the series
to be prepared for publication. It has not yet been published, but I am confident that when the moment is right,
it will be.

Over the next two years, I found myself impelled by a
desire to share about the angels with others. I sought out
existing avenues, like national angel-interest clubs, and
corresponded with the authors of angel books and music.
I searched the media for references to angels and noted
what the emphases seemed to be. And two things became
very clear:

First, even the people who were most involved in this
angel-awareness phenomenon didn't seem to realize or
be able to communicate the enormity of the phenomenon. Each was isolated from the others by geography or
inclination or medium of expression.

Second, as I already knew in my own life, I could also see a fundamental difference in the way angels were at work in the world today in comparison with what I knew of their involvement in the past.

I decided at that point that what was needed was some sort of a clearinghouse for information about the angels. It would be an angel watch, not to focus attention on the angels themselves, which they hate, but so that we would be reminded of the God of love at whose command these beings come forth to serve and to help us find our way with ever-increasing speed toward the Light. Help, assistance, necessary publicity, and even some small monetary contributions helped me to get The Angel-Watch Network off the ground. I am not a preacher by nature, but *AngelWatch* is how I witness publicly that our God is a loving God who cares intimately about each of us, even giving us into the care of our angel guardians, who lead us toward love and wisdom and away from fear and hate.

I believe in angels.

Chapter Two

Who Are Angels?

hen we use the word *angel*, we have a certain image in mind that is based on our cultural and religious beliefs. For the average person, an angel is a being with wings and a halo, generally quite beautiful, of great age and wisdom, who comes from a place called heaven and occasionally appears on earth.

Some believe that angels are different from humans; some feel that angels are humans who have been transformed or perfected in the afterlife. There are those who view angels as ideas of God or merely literary devices. Because angels seem to exist in another dimension or mode of being than our own, much of what we say about angels is speculation based on revered traditions held to be sacred or personal intuition/revelation.

The sacred books of many of the world's great religious systems speak of angels: Judaism, Christianity, Islam, Zoroastrianism, to name some of the major ones. Many other religious scriptures describe beings who are comparable to the beings our society calls angels. Some religions and philosophies believe in more than one kind of spirit intermediate between us humans and God.

One thing is clear: Angels are far more than projections of the divine mind or literary devices. They are real, personal beings, even if their corporeality is totally different from ours. Literary devices and mythical beings cannot touch people's lives and utterly transform them. Ancient stories and legends are not capable of changing tires for stranded motorists before disappearing. Angels are beings, creatures, as we are, but different.

For me, the simplest explanation of who angels are is also the one most easily seen in the light of the ancient texts that first speak of them: *Angels are another race of sentient, intelligent beings, different from humans, far more ancient and powerful, wiser and more evolved.* I believe that angels were created by God to serve the divine, not only in the worship that is spoken of in all scriptures, but in helping to form and keep in existence our world and other heavenly bodies. Angels have their own society and values, hierarchy and activities. They have consciousness and will and purpose. They are organized to achieve goals and to grow in consciousness. In many of these things they are not so different from us—we, too, are societal creatures with will and purpose, who grow. But there is a fundamental difference between us.

Angels are not a society of glorified human beings. They do not represent the ultimate growth potential of the human spirit. Not a single human being has ever become or will ever become an angel, no matter how pure or holy or evolved he or she might grow to be. Do oak trees evolve into giraffes? Can a mountain (which for all I know might have consciousness) become a beluga whale if given enough time? Can oxygen evolve into a cat? No, each is a unique type of creation, and while each may change or grow, it does so according to the natural laws that govern its species. The ancient writings are clear that angels are a separate species, one that predates the appearance of the human race. (I believe quite firmly that human beings have a destiny and an evolutionary potential that is far more glorious than that of angels, but that is a subject for another book.) We and the angels are on parallel tracks as far as our development is concerned.

Actually, the view that people can become angels after they leave this world is fairly recent, as beliefs go. Some scholars trace one strand of this belief to the great plagues that swept Europe during the late Middle Ages. During that period, infants and children were particularly vulnerable, and it was comforting for grieving parents to think of their loved ones as becoming happy little angels no longer in need of comfort, who could come back to earth in turn to comfort the parents. (The first artwork depicting angels as chubby little children with wings also dates from this era.)

Today the view that angels are humans who have "died-and-gone-to-heaven" is most clearly perpetuated in the American pop culture, in which movies like *It's a Wonderful Life* and songs like "Teen Angel," with their stories of humans who come back to earth as angels, only serve to confuse the issue. Add to this the fact that the term *guardian angel* has become a synonym for any human being who is especially helpful in a moment of crisis, and the possibilities for confusion are multiplied.

In fact, in writing this book, I received several stories from people who believed that their deceased loved ones were now acting as their guardian angels and had saved them from same dangerous situations. While I am sure that those who loved us on earth continue to do so after they have left this world, they do not become angels in order to do so. I prefer to think of them as working with our particular guardian angels in whatever ways God permits, but as human beings. After all, what is so menial about being human that we feel we must be transformed into angels in order to achieve our greatest growth and develoment? According to the Christian scriptures, the destiny of human beings exceeds that of the angels by an indefinably great margin. Human beings will "judge" angels, a phrase some interpret to mean that human society on the other side of death is so wonderful that it is superior to the angels'. And in Islam the fallen angels were banished from paradise when God ordered them to bow down to Adam. Iblis was the chief of those who refused, saying that he would not prostrate before a creature made of mud.

Angels in Heaven

The beings we call *angels* have been the subject of serious human speculation for thousands of years. Our present generation is far from the first to be interested in these beings and to want to know more about them. When men and women first came to write down their religious beliefs nearly five thousand years ago, their accounts of how the cosmos came to exist, angels—although under other names—were already an accepted reality. (The difficulty for us modern people is that unless a creature from antiquity has wings and a halo and acts in ways we associate with angels, we are reluctant to recognize them as such.)

We can read in the creation story that was known to every Babylonian child nearly five thousand years ago that the great gods had a council of lesser beings to help them, to carry their messages, to protect mountains and towns and special people on earth. These lesser beings, called the "sons of the gods," were immortal beings but not gods themselves. Clearly older and more powerful than human beings, they went about the business of heaven according to the will of the gods on high. Ancient societies worshipped the beings we would call angels as though they were divine.

In time, this rather primitive view of the angels as lesser gods was modified—no doubt to the great relief of the angels themselves! The ancient Jews, whose ideas of angels have shaped the beliefs of most people today, were among the first to truly see that divinity could not be parceled out like red hair or Roman noses among so many squabbling gods and goddesses, but was a uniqueness that was indivisible. The beings who made up the "council of the gods" they saw instead as creatures who served and obeyed God, who lived in another dimension than earth, and whose connection with the earth was largely confined to offering advice when requested. They were still sometimes called the "sons of God" or the "holy Ones," but it was clear that they were not thought of as being really God's offspring in some kind of "biological" sense.

Nor were the ancient Jews alone in this understanding. In Persia, a native religion of great importance developed that also saw a supreme benevolent god surrounded by a court of lesser spirits who provided counsel and assistance in the maintaining of the world and the life on it. In this system, Ahura Mazda, the Wise Lord, was served by beings called the Amesha Spentas, who in terms of powers and functions are very similar to the beings that we call archangels. The religion of Zoroaster is an ancient one, still practiced today, particularly in some areas of India and Iran.

So, in one sense, the angels of antiquity were seen as shadowy beings who inhabited the realm of God or the gods, and had little contact with the world.

Angels on Earth

However, running parallel to this track is another one, virtually as ancient, in which certain angels come to earth frequently and interact with human beings for their benefit.

From the beginning of recorded history, special men and women were written of as having been given their own heavenly protectors, who sometimes even fought each other for the benefit of their wards or protégés. Nations had their own guardian gods, some greater, some lesser, as did the various city-states and towns. Still lesser guardians watched over wells and springs, over cattle and fish and date palms. In fact, the whole concept that we humans have of our advocates and heavenly guardians is so ancient that no one knows how early it began.

I have always felt, with the great psychologist Carl Jung, that some ideas are so basic to our orientation as human beings that they are part of the collective unconscious, racial memories, as it were, things we've known and believed for so long that they are set into our brain cells from the moment they come into being, a kind of organic Read Only Memory (ROM). Such instinctive memories include the universal belief that animals and plants are living, in a different category of existence from the inanimate world.

Are There Different Kinds of Angels?

Whether there are different species or races of angels, or whether all angels are the same "under the skin" but simply have different functions or duties has never been settled. Are angels fundamentally different from archangels, like gorillas and humans, or is it more accurate to describe angels as "rank and file" and archangels as "management" within the same species? We don't know. For every person who has had an insight or claimed a revelation in one direction, another person has felt the opposite. (For a discussion of the various orders of angels and their functions, see Chapter Three.)

The question of whether angels have gender is also open to discussion. When angels appear before our eyes, they usually suggest the masculine or feminine. But they probably do this to give us points of reference we are familiar with. Many people have been touched by angels who appeared neither one nor the other, and those who know their angels heart to heart rather than face-to-face usually do not have a sense of gender about their angels at all.

Such a feeling, however, may come from the possibility that angelic genders are so totally unlike the two we know on earth that we just can't recognize the concept in angels. Some philosophers have even speculated that every angel is a separate gender, a different physical and spiritual orientation to life.

For myself, I believe that angels have genders, which may include the two we know on earth and others. I believe that everything that exists has gender, in the way that Eastern thought sees everything in the cosmos in terms of yin or yang, a basic orientation toward existence. English is one of the world's languages in which nouns are not classified grammatically as masculine or feminine (or neuter or dual). This makes it harder for us to see how the concept of gender pervades the universe. Most languages—Hebrew, Sanskrit, French, Russian, German, Arabic—assign genders to all nouns, even those describing inanimate objects, and some even assign genders to verbs, making some actions masculine, some feminine.

One of the most interesting discussions of angelic genders can be found in C. S. Lewis's space trilogy. The second volume, *Perelandra*, offers, in fictional format, a wealth of intuitive speculation about the genders of angels.

What Do Angels Look Like?

The fact is, we don't know what angels look like. All we know is what they look like to us.

This may seem surprising, but it's true. Everyone who has had an angelic encounter has seen something different from everyone else who has seen or experienced an angel. There is nothing absolutely consistent, no one theme that runs through all the angel encounters that have ever been reported. And, in any case, what we see with our human eyes is only a gift from the angels themselves, an approximation, a translation of one reality to another. And, as the Italian proverb goes, *Traduttore, traditore,* Every translator is a betrayer. It can't be helped—any angel we see or sense or hear is only a translation of the original.

But even if we don't know for certain, there are some tantalizing hints, some interesting similarities, and if we look at the kinds of experiences people have had, we may draw some interesting conclusions about what angels may "look" like.

Eileen Elias Freeman

Pretty Little Angel Eyes?

What are angels' bodies really like? Do they even have bodies? Are they physical organisms? Do they depend on air and light, on nourishment of some kind? Do they see? Do they hear? Can they touch and taste?

We have to make a distinction here between the way angels appear to each other, in the dimension where they normally exist, the dimension we humans generally call heaven, and how angels look to us when we are permitted a glimpse of them. Since we do not have angelic "eyes," it is not really possible for us to say what angels look like to other angels. As a result of scientific experiments, we can create approximate models of what the world looks like to a bee or a cat or a dragonfly, but we cannot do this with angels—we cannot examine them under a microscope.

The general consensus of scholarly opinion is that angels do not have bodies in the way all life on earth has form. All on earth, from humans, to the giant redwood trees, to clouds, have bodies whose forms have been dictated by the fact that all exist on a particular type of planet, with a certain gravity, with various climates and terrains. And there are wide differences, even within species, who have had to survive in different parts of the world. When I lived in Arizona, I often saw jackrabbits bounding along through the brush, their enormous ears sticking upright. The size of the ears, I was told, enabled them to release body heat in the desert climate. But the snowshoe hares of the Arctic have tiny ears to save heat, because they developed in a different world. If we had evolved on Mars, for example, we might have had taller or thinner bodies, and maybe we would have had giant ears ourselves to cup the sound waves in the thin air. If we came from Jupiter, perhaps the immense gravity on that planet would have caused us to flow along the ground rather than stand upright. So even in the physical universe, we understand that all creatures are the physical products of their environment.

But what environment is native to the angels? Most of those who have studied about angels believe that angels do not live in the same physical universe as we do at all. They may call it heaven or a parallel universe, or something else. In any case, angels come through a sort of doorway, whether physical or mental, to make themselves known to us. Jacob's vision of the stairway that reached to heaven and by means of which angels descended to earth is a good example of this belief. John writes in Revelation 4, "I saw an open door to heaven," and he was caught up in ecstasy at the sight of God and the angels. This view of the cosmos generally says that angels are beings of pure spirit and have no physical bodies at all. They have no faces, no hands, no wings, no auras, because there is no body to base them on. They are pure spirit, as God is spirit, without any corporeality at all.

But there is another theory that is gaining ground today: that angels do indeed live in the same physical universe we do, but that their bodies, whatever they may be like, are simply of a sort that we cannot see. Such a concept would not have been truly possible in ancient days. Until quite recently, the existence of physical bodies we cannot see with our eyes would have been deemed heresy in many parts of the world. When epidemics of plague or typhoid or other diseases swept away the populations of towns and cities, no one dreamed that the cause could be a life form with a microscopically small body, too small for anyone to even know the existence of. No one suspected that all matter was made up of infinitesimally small bits of matter called atoms, or that these atoms were made of even smaller bits. Even today, modern science is still discovering new subatomic particles.

That angels should be a part of our own cosmos, but unseen because their bodies are different from ours, is the possibility that seems most likely to me. Why should we think that we are the ultimate species here on earth? Why shouldn't we share this part of the universe with other intelligent beings? We acknowledge that there are life forms we cannot see with our eyes; why shouldn't angels be another life form of this nature, immensely older, wiser, more loving?

Heavenly Bodies?

But what can we usefully speculate about angelic form? Here are some of the most frequently argued theories about what angelic bodies may be like and why we don't see them.

Popular in today's science fiction novels and television are characters called shape-shifters, beings made up primarily of energy, who can transform themselves into anything. We know that angels can and do perform these sorts of transformations, appearing now as different human beings or animals, looking more or less human. Perhaps angelic bodies are like that—made up of a kind of very fluid energy that our sensors, our radar, and other tracking devices haven't been able to identify.

Or perhaps angels do have physical bodies of some sort, but they move too fast for us to see them. I remember an old episode of *Star Trek* from my youth, in which the crew of the *Enterprise* couldn't communicate with the inhabitants of a world they visited, because the creatures on this planet moved at such speed that the human eyes of the crew couldn't catch them. Even on earth, ordinary things of our world can move too fast for us to see. (If I'm not concentrating, my cats can zip past me so quickly I can't tell which of them is running the Indy 500 in my living room.) Suppose angels move at the speed of light, as they are beings of light and servants of the Light? Such a concept goes back at least to biblical times. In Daniel 9:21, Gabriel comes to the prophet "in rapid flight at the time of the evening sacrifice." In Daniel 14:33, Habakkuk the prophet is taken from Judea to Babylon by an angel who transports him "with the speed of the wind." And Psalm 104 records, "Like the winds, your angels go before you."

Or suppose angels have physical bodies, but our eyes aren't sensitive enough to see them. It's true that our eyes can see a wide spectrum of light between ultraviolet and infrared; it's also true that many animals and insects can see ultraviolet and infrared, which we cannot. The centers of some flowers fluoresce under an ultraviolet lamp. Bees can see this special color and home in on the source of nectar, while, to us, the entire flower looks to be white or another color. Maybe angels' bodies exist in color spectra our eyes just can't see.

And as a result, perhaps their communications to us are in a medium we can't hear. For example, at this moment, no matter where you are, your ears are being invaded by radio waves. The same currents are passing right through your body, titillating your brain, and teasing your body. Do you hear the music? No, because our bodies don't have an interpreter, a decoder. But the minute you turn on your radio, these radio waves representing perhaps hundreds of different signals—songs, talk shows, speeches, news—are all available to your ears. And you never stop to think that these radio waves are all around you and in you.

Perhaps angels' bodies are totally transparent. There are creatures on this planet with transparent bodies or parts of bodies. And there are many substances on earth that are transparent, like glass, mica, clear quartz crystal, raindrops, the wind. Suppose angelic bodies simply do not reflect any kind of light and are thus invisible to our eyes.

Perhaps angels' beings are more tenuous than our own. Our bodies are dense and have weight. Suppose the substance of an angel's being is light and spread out. For example: We look at a tapestry and we see the whole pattern of a unicorn hunt from the Middle Ages. But suppose the same scene was played out on a tapestry ten thousand miles wide, or suppose the tapestry stayed the same, but we were reduced to an inch in height. Would we see the pattern? Would we even recognize the whole as a tapestry? No, we would be reaching out to touch a single thread that seemed to us like the braided cable of a suspension bridge. So perhaps our external sight is too limited to see the vast pattern that might be an angel's being.

I suspect that the biggest reason why we don't know what an angel's physical being is like is because our internal sight is too limited. Jesus said, "Look! The Kingdom of God is all around you, in your very midst." I have always felt that he meant that even though our human senses, physical and spiritual, aren't sensitive enough to see and know God directly, or even the angelic servants of God or those we love who have gone before us, nonetheless, what we call heaven and earth are separated by far less than we think. If our lives were utterly pure and filled with light and love, we would find no barrier between the dimension we live in and that of the angels. We would see them constantly. We would see the face of God unveiled, and it would consume and transform us totally and all around us. If we could only "Look!"

Of course no one is that perfect. But in the history of the human race, many men and women have achieved the kind of enlightenment and understanding that have permitted them to walk with the angels from time to time. And there are others of enormous innocence who have also walked with the angels.

So we have to admit that whatever kinds of physical attributes angels may have in their own dimension, we are not normally capable of seeing and comprehending them. And when we do encounter them, whether they visit us in our dimension or whether God enraptures us into that of the angels, our own senses are not adequate to describe with great accuracy and precision what we have seen. This brings us to the question of how angels appear to us and why they assume the forms they do.

Why Do Angels Have Wings?

They don't—not really.

We have always portrayed angels as ethereal humanlike beings, because we have no other way to depict them. We are limited by the world around us and by our inability to translate into human language the supernatural events we often experience. In the Judaeo-Christian scriptures, most of the very books that speak the loudest about angels—Daniel and Revelation—are the ones in which the writer is relating the contents of visions and dreams, where everyday language is useless to describe things that are not of this dimension. Those who have been touched by angels must speak in metaphor or speak not at all. And even human metaphor is grossly inadequate for the task.

An angel's wings are the quintessential proof of how poor the language of even the most eloquent orator is when describing a vision.

Whatever their physical appearance, angels do not have heavier-than-air bodies. They do not fly through air in order to get from point A to point B. Given their inherent power, they can be anywhere they want in an instant, or so we humans have believed for thousands of years. The idea of bird wings on angels is just not reality.

In fact, the earliest representations or literary descriptions of angels do not show them with wings. If you remember Jacob's vision, the angels who were ascending to and descending from heaven used a ladder, hardly the kind of equipment that beings with wings would need. The angels who came to Abraham showed no evidence of wings. In fact throughout the Judaeo-Christian scriptures, the only angelic creatures portrayed with wings are the cherubim and seraphim, and as most people know, the Hebrew artisan's model for the cherubim was the Babylonian keribbu, a protecting deity part human and part bird. The seraphim of Isaiah 6 also have wings. We are used to seeing paintings showing a sky filled with winged, flying angels singing to the shepherds on the night of Jesus' birth. And yet there is no reference in Matthew or Luke to such an event. Certainly the gospels speak of the herald angel and the multitude of angels who sang their hymn of joy, but nothing about wings. Maybe they stood all around the shepherds on the plain or hillside and filled them with their song. Perhaps they gathered in a great circle around the sheep and danced as they sang. We certainly don't know. But if they elected to dance or sing in the air, they did so without wings.

Angel-like beings in many other ancient Near Eastern religions are similarly wing-less.

So why does most art depict angels with wings? Actually, angels were not depicted in art, specifically Christian art, a great deal until after 787 of the common era. In that year the second Council of Nicaea, a great church council, decreed that it was lawful to depict images of angels and saints in art. This leashed an explosion of paintings, sculptures, and illuminations over the next five centuries. But artists, coming to paint angels for the first time, had virtually no models to go by. The stories from the Bible told them that angels often looked quite human; the theology of the day told them that angels were really sexless beings made of spirit, who could be anywhere at once.

So artists turned toward the only models they knew— those of the Greek and Latin classical sculptors and paint- ers, who were accustomed to portraying Mercury (or Hermes), the messenger of the gods, with wings, either on his sandals or on his helmet. Other winged creatures were Nike, the symbol of victory, and Eros, the god of love. All of these winged figures went into the making of the angel in art. And as far as the portrayal of the wings was concerned, medieval artists used the only models available—birds, and especially birds considered wonder- ful or admirable, like the swan and the eagle.

But many people have had encounters with winged angels, it can be argued. It is true that when men and women see angels today, they often see them with wings. Since angels do not have wings, does it mean that all these people are imagining things? No, not at all. Any time an angel makes itself known to us, all we are ever going to see is an appearance, an approximation of what that angel really is. In fact, the angel is going to appear to us in whatever way it feels is most calculated to draw our attention, to listen to its message, and to act upon it. If an angel feels we will be most attentive to a being that looks like the models we are accustomed to seeing in art, it will use such a model and build on it. Keep in mind that long before angels appeared to people with wings, they were still awesome enough that they had to tell us not to be afraid.

This type of visitation in the form of what we expect to see, rather than what is, is not uncommon. The best other example is Jesus himself. Many people over the centuries have claimed that Jesus has appeared to them, and that they have seen the wounds in his feet and side, and in the palms of his hands. But we have learned through modern archaeology that Roman crucifixion nailed the person's hands through the wrists, where several bones met, and the nail would not rip out. So throughout the centuries, artists' representations of the crucifixion have been anatomically incorrect. Were all these visionaries hysterics?

The answer once again is no. In fact, a medieval mystic, Saint Brigid, saw such a vision of Jesus; then, while meditating upon its meaning for her, she saw Jesus' mother, who told her that Jesus had looked that way to her because that is what her eyes expected. "My son's hands were more firmly fixed," she said, pointing out what the science of archaeology discovered centuries later. In the twentieth century, the stigmatic Therese Neumann had a comparable experience.

I might also point out that when angels take on a human appearance to help us or bring us messages, they never have wings. In fact, there is virtually nothing to distinguish them from any one of us.

Halo, Everyone

Do angels have halos, those golden circles of light around their heads?

Here the answer is most definitely yes, and even more than aureoles of light. Angels' whole beings, when they appear in our lives, are filled with light that overflows and colors our world, and I feel that even when the encounters are heart to heart their light reaches out to our spirits.

I have read hundreds and hundreds of personal encounters between the angels and us. In most of those cases where an angel has not deliberately taken on a fully human appearance, the angel is bathed in light that the person who has seen the angel cannot describe adequately. They use many similes and metaphors and approximations to try to convey what the light was like.

- "It was like a bright white, but it was brighter than any white I've ever seen."
- "It was like iridescent, like mother-of-pearl, but it was transparent."
- "There were colors I've never seen on earth and don't ever expect to see."
- "If a diamond were made of silver and the light of the sun and moon were shining from behind . . ."
- "It was a kind of golden pink that faded along the edges to a sort of silvery white that appeared to shimmer."
- "If sunlight were blue and full of glitter—but it was really night with a full moon, that's sort of what it was like."

These are descriptions of how some people I have spoken with have seen an angelic aura. Far from just surrounding the head of the angel, the unearthly light glowed from within and surrounded the being in glory.

Some people reported not being able to look the angel in the eyes at first, until they had gotten used to the light.

But this phenomenon is not confined to the modern era. One sees it in many ancient texts such as Enoch, and in the Judaeo-Christian scriptures as well:

● His body was like chrysolite, his face shone like lightning, his eyes were like fiery torches. . . . (Daniel 10:6)

● In appearance (the angel) resembled a flash of lightning, while his garments were as dazzling as snow. (Matthew 28:3)

● At three o'clock I was at home praying when a man in dazzling robes stood before me. (Acts 10:30)

Artists tended to confine the aura or halo to the face and head for several reasons:

1) Christian iconography developed different kinds of halos for Christ, the Virgin, saints, and angels. In some periods it was preferable to use conventional imagery than to develop new representations.

2) With many figures overlapping, a large aura would have obscured details of the painting, so the halo was cut down.

3) Real gold, which was often used to create the halo, was expensive, and limiting the halo also limited the expense.

4) As creatures of thought, angels were revered for their intelligence and intellectual prowess; therefore, the head, which for us humans is the center of that function, was highlighted.

There are many exceptions, of course, particularly as art was freed from having to be approved by ecclesiastical authorities. Modern artists who have been touched by angels themselves are painting these heavenly messengers in very different guise than in centuries before, depicting the strength, fluidity, sense of purpose, and love the angels show. But in the case of the angelic aura or halo, this is one case where art has captured, however poorly, the divine light that fills these glorious beings who come to touch our lives with the love of God.

Unity in Diversity

What can we extrapolate about what angels look like from the thousands of encounters that people have reported?

Angelic appearances run a wide gamut from beings that appear just like other humans to creatures who hover just on the edge of invisibility. As I have said, they adopt whatever form will enable them to do what is necessary for us.

When angels appear as human beings, they do so in order to act in disguise. For this reason we can never tell at a given moment that the person we have been with is an angel. They come as humans so they *won't* be recognized. It's only afterward when we ask the question, *Was that an angel?* And we don't ask the question because of something we noted about them at that time, but because of something they did or said or caused or prevented, and often because as soon as they were finished they simply disappeared or vanished. The vanishing angel is a common motif in people's encounters.

Just as often, angels appear in something less than a fully human form. When I was a child, I saw part of a humanlike creature overflowing with light. When an angel only takes on a partly human appearance, it does so because the fiction of a human encounter is not necessary. Perhaps for some reason it is essential to make the supernatural nature of the event especially important. Would I have believed a strange human being who came to my room (when I was afraid of burglars and bogeys anyway)? I know I wouldn't.

Sometimes people report that they saw their angel, but what they saw was simply the light or aura itself; they did not see even the hint of a figure within the light. This happens, too; when the encounter is of this nature, it is often true that the person receiving it is either used to such appearances, or has a quality of inner vision that makes a more humanlike encounter unnecessary.

It also happens that people hear their angel speak to them or feel their touch without seeing anything. This happened to me when I was in college, and although the encounter was brief, I knew it at once for the work of my guardian angel Enniss. I suspect that these encounters where there is virtually nothing physical are either designed just to get a person's attention so some fuller contact can be made in the future, or are meant for people who don't need such physical experiences of angels.

A special kind of angelic encounter comes during a near-death experience. Andy Lakey, whose story is told in Chapter Ten, had such an encounter. Apart from the fact that it took place in the "corridor" that joins our earthly dimension with the heavenly, the appearance was not unlike the more ethereal visions people see in this plane. I think the reason for this is that someone near death still perceives things with the senses he or she has always known. They have not shaken off their body; some part of their physical being accompanies them when they journey temporarily to the borders of the great Kingdom.

Tongues of Angels

How do angels speak? What language do they use? Or do they even use language as we understand it?

The essence of the angels who come to us is the ability to communicate perfectly with us, to convey their messages clearly and unambiguously. How do they do this?

It is clear from the experiences of many people who have been touched by angels that they communicate spiritually or telepathically—mind speaking to mind, without the intermediary of a voice. I know that in 1979, when my angels began communicating the concepts I came to put into *The Pilot Program*, that by far the majority of our conversation was other than oral. I have heard from quite a number of individuals who received strong messages from their angels without seeing them speak.

Angels, being creatures of vast intellect, know all our human languages, but among themselves how do they communicate? Various mystical books, most of them coming out of Judaeo-Christian influences (for example, *The Book of the Angel Raziel*) purport to contain whole angelic alphabets. (Several are reproduced in Gustav Davidson's *A Dictionary of Angels*.) But these should surely be taken as the magico-mystical devices that they are.

Saint Paul says in 1 Corinthians 13:1, "If I speak in tongues, whether they are human or angelic, but have no love, I am no better than a clanging gong or a clashing cymbal." Clearly, he believed that angels had their own languages, and that even humans, under divine inspiration, could speak them.

But I think that Paul was waxing a bit poetic. Common sense tells us that angels do not have bodies like ours, nor are they dependent on a world like ours. They have no need to draw breath, and they have no lips, no larynx, no tongue to form speech. Whatever their means of communication among themselves, it cannot be in language such as we use.

But when they touch us with their presence, they communicate flawlessly.

Chapter Three
What Do Angels Do?

lthough we only know tantalizing bits about it, it is clear that the angels who touch our lives live in a well-ordered, highly disciplined society. They are not mindless, aimless, solitary cloud-dwellers, but social beings with purpose, responsibilities, duties, and the need to cooperate and work together.

This is a side of angelic life that we rarely are permitted to see. Although we may be touched by our angels, it is most usual for the contact to be one-on-one. But there have been enough thinkers and visionaries whose hearts or eyes have pierced the barrier that separates the angelic world from the human that we know some things about what angels actually do and how they are organized.

The Society of Angels

"God is a God of order, not of confusion," the Christian scriptures say. And this is true. All around us we can see the fruits of the divine order. Matter is organized into particles, particles into atoms, atoms into bodies—and each body behaves according to natural laws established within those atoms. Cats look like cats; they have claws and eat meat. Asphalt is black, doesn't eat anything, and only moves when it melts in the heat of the summer. None of this is by chance.

Even before the structure of matter was understood, humankind understood that part of the nature of the divine is to order things. At the beginning of Genesis, it says of the nascent earth, "And the earth was a formless waste, and darkness covered the face of the abyss." And then what happens? The Spirit of God (also translatable as "a mighty wind" or even "the divine breath") quickens the world and, one by one, its features are separated out of the chaos and given form, structure, and purpose: the light, the dark, the heavenly bodies, the features of the earth and its creatures.

And the biblical creation account does not stand alone. Throughout the ancient world, the idea that the divine brings order out of chaos because it hates confusion is prevalent. The Babylonian story, called the *Enuma Elish*, describes the same process. The Egyptian account tells of the gods of Egypt setting up the banks of the Nile, the date palms, and the society of humankind. China, Japan, Mesoamerica, and Polynesia all have creation stories in which the divine orders the mundane.

For this reason alone, if for no other, we must realize that angelic society is an ordered society, in which an immense number of beings work and cooperate together. It could not be otherwise. Common enterprises like worship of God or more societal efforts like the "war in heaven," when angels fought together to drive out those who "fell," could never have been possible without the order of cooperation.

Throughout human history, a few visionaries have been allowed a glimpse into angelic society, and they all testify to the perfect order and ensuing harmony of angelic society. Most have to use metaphor and obscure language to describe their visions, because angelic society and organization is not like ours, but they all agree that heaven is a society with purpose. The Revelation of Saint John is full of such descriptions, from glorious and complex accounts of divine worship to angelic visits to earth. Isaiah the prophet had a vision of God and the angelic court, and the perfection of it almost caused him to despair of human society by comparison. "I am doomed!" he cries. "Here I am, with all my wickedness, living in a wicked society, and I have just seen the Lord of the heavenly host!" Many other ancient works—*Esdras*, *Enoch*, the *Assumption of Moses*—offer visions into angelic society.

All testify that the society of angels is virtually a perfect one in itself. No dissension, no jealousy, no burning ambition, no violence mar its surface. No one is preferred, no one left out. All know their gifts and abilities and responsibilities, and all work ceaselessly to perfect them and to be faithful to their duties. All have unlimited scope for growth, and all have "hearts" immovably fixed upon God. The only law is the law of love.

Whether angels were created this way, or whether they evolved a perfect society over uncounted eons we simply do not know. For myself, I believe to a certain extent that they evolved. After all, the literature of revelation is full of stories of a period when a kind of civil war broke out in heaven, until Michael and many other angels combined to drive out those angels who apparently did not want to live according to the "rules" of angelic society.

And besides this, it is the nature of all life forms that they grow and evolve. Change occurs far more rapidly in this world than in the angels' realm; but even so, I am sure that angels are not static beings, created with a finite set of instructions and knowledge. Perhaps in comparison with our intellect theirs seem vast, but they learn and grow, too.

Angels are not affected personally by the pain and evil that still exist on earth. They have a much greater vision than we, and they know that in time, as we seek the ways of Love and Light, we will grow beyond such things. However, one thing does affect them—when we mistakenly think of them as substitutes for the Light, as mini-gods, as beings to be worshipped or placated. For an angel, this is as close to pain as is possible.

The Orders of Angels

In any human society, the members of that society have different jobs to do, different roles to play. This is also true of angelic society, and speculation about their work has created a large body of literature on that subject alone. But with angels the question is more complicated than with humans. All humans belong to the same race. Some speculate that angels do not, that archangels are a different "race" from seraphim, who are a different race from cherubim. The word *angel* is both the generic word we use of any celestial being and the name of yet another "race."

I'm not sure whether I believe this is so. As one reads the ancient literature, different angels like Michael, Raphael, Gabriel, Uriel, and others are described as belonging to various orders of angels. It seems more logical to me that angels should be called upon to change their function than the nature of their beings.

Speculation on the different groups angels belong to, either by type of being or function, has remained constant for about the last twenty-seven hundred years. In Western tradition, the earliest distinctions are in the Hebrew scriptures, where the celestial beings are called messengers, sons of God, cherubim, and seraphim. The messengers are those angels who come to earth and interact with humans. The sons of God are angels who make up the heavenly court and are not particularly concerned with matters terrestrial. The cherubim, who derive from a Babylonian model, have several different appearances: First, they are winged creatures in art, upon which the ark of the covenant on earth, and the throne of God in heaven, rest. Second, they are celestial beings in ancient Hebrew prophecy, particularly in Ezekiel. Third, they have special functions as guardians; in Genesis 4 the cherubim guard the way to the tree of life, and in Ezekiel 28, a cherub is assigned as guardian to the first man until the man does evil and the cherub drives him from the mountain of God (although addressed to the king of Tyre, this story is actually an alternate creation story). The seraphim, winged, like the cherubim, worship before the throne of God.

This four-part distinction of angelic orders or functions gradually changed and expanded. In the book of Daniel, Michael and others are called Princes, and are clearly special protective beings whose function is to watch over nations. (Perhaps this term is the same as archangel, for in the letter of Jude, Michael is referred to as an archangel.) There is also a category of celestials called the Watchers, who carry out divine commands on earth. In *Tobit*, the angel Raphael calls himself one of the Seven who stand before the throne of God.

In other contemporary literature, the orders of angels and their tasks are described in incredible detail. The book of Enoch is especially noteworthy in naming a myriad of angels, together with their heavenly functions. It would take a book just to present all the angels and groups of angels in Enoch alone.

By the beginning of the Christian era, between seven and twelve groups of angelic functions or beings had been identified by a number of theologians. Paul talks about "thrones, dominations, principalities and powers" in Colossians 1:16. Ambrose, Jerome, Gregory the Great, Clement, and Pseudo-Dionysius all had their groups. Medieval Jewish scholars speculated no less, and the systems of the Zohar and others are just as complex and contradictory as those of Christian scholars.

The system propounded by Pseudo-Dionysius in the fourth century of the common era is the one that has achieved the most fame. Highest in rank are the seraphim, cherubim, and thrones. These three orders of angels provide ceaseless worship around the throne of God and act as the heavenly council. Next in rank are the dominions, virtues, and powers, who govern the functions of the cosmos. Third are principalities, archangels, and angels, who act as guardians to humanity, as well as to nations, cities, groups, other life forms, and things. Whether this system is any truer than others is uncertain, but it is the one that most scholars have accepted over the centuries.

All of these systems testify to the belief that the angelic world is extremely well organized. It would have to be— visionaries who have seen through the curtain tell of uncounted numbers of heavenly beings—myriads upon myriads. Chaos would result if angels did not know their places and responsibilities.

What Do Angels Do?

The servants of God do whatever God asks of them. And it appears that angels are asked to do an immense variety of things. From literature we see that, in general, this includes:

Worshipping God

All angels worship God. This is clearly their most basic function—to reflect back to God the glory of creation.

It is also why people who are accustomed to worshipping God more often achieve the kind of heart-to-heart contact with their angels that so many people desire—they share the same deep interest as the angels. In the visions of Isaiah and John, both hear the words and songs of the angels' worship, which they describe as going on ceaselessly. I believe that no matter what kind of special mission an angel may be performing, even on earth, that the angel's heart is always absorbed in contemplation of the divine, and I think that the angelic aura reflects that state of constant worship.

Bringing messages to earth or ministering to humans on earth

Angels often come to earth on special missions to bring messages from God. And such angels need not be guardian angels, just because they interact with humanity. Gabriel brought messages of enormous import to the prophet Daniel, to Zachary, and to Mary the mother of Jesus, but Gabriel is not generally viewed as a guardian angel. The angels who ministered to Jesus during his retreat to the desert were not guardian angels.

Guarding the heavenly realms from the fallen angels

The concept of the Heavenly Host, God's angelic army, is an ancient one. In biblical times this army was seen as fighting invisibly for those who were in the right. And in Daniel and Revelation clear mention is made of Michael and his angels who throw the rebellious angels bodily out of the space or ambiance or whatever one calls it that is heaven. We don't know much about this heavenly warfare or whether it goes on today. Perhaps all around us the angels of God are boldly fighting the angels of darkness for the Kingdom.

Helping to maintain the natural functions of the world and the cosmos

Angels are also set in place to watch over natural phenomena and the governance of the earth and other heavenly bodies. According to some angelologists and mystics, every blade of grass has its angel to watch over it. And the grass itself has an even higher angel over it. And other angels watch over the plant realm and the world and the solar system. Jewish mystical literature from the Middle Ages on down has multiplied the names of angels in incredible detail. Every virtue, every human event, every day, week, minute, year has its own angel. I am not sure that all of this is so, literally, but it is certain that angels do watch over the world as a whole.

Serving as spiritual and even physical guardians to humanity—individually and in groups

Every person who has ever lived on this planet has had an angel guardian to watch over them. This is a commonly held belief, known to Judaism, Christianity,

Islam, Zoroastrianism, and many other religions. It is spoken of in orthodox scriptures as well as in complementary writings and mystical works.

But what does a guardian angel do? My own belief is that our angels are assigned to us at conception, not at birth. They are rather like spiritual godparents or sponsors, and they work to raise our level of spiritual awareness throughout our lives. They speak to our hearts constantly as one channel by which God graces our beings, and they ceaselessly whisper to us of love and peace, and wholeness and how to work toward those goals.

The term "guardian angel" is not directly from any scriptures, or even from collateral literature. It is a phrase that we ourselves have developed to describe the angels who work with us on this earth, based on Psalm 91: "He has given his angels charge over you, to guard you in all your ways. Upon their hands they will bear you up, lest you dash your foot against a stone."

But what do angels guard? My own feeling is that their principal work lies with our spirits, not with our bodies. They are the guardians of our souls, our heart of hearts. I believe that they intervene in our physical world when such intervention is necessary to enrich or deliver our spirits. But in all they do, they are givers, providers, facilitators; they are not generals, bosses, commanders. They work with us, not upon us or against us. Their society is not ordered along the lines of orders, punishments and rewards, so they do not give us orders or disturb our free will. We can cooperate with their advice and suggestions, and if we are wise, we will, but we can ignore them, if we choose to.

I believe that we each have one principal guardian

angel, but that our angel may have many others to assist. In Islam it is believed that a recording angel assists our guardians by taking note of all our good deeds (and the reverse). And we may have other angels who watch over us for other reasons. Martha Powers, who tells her story in this book, says she had a special angel over her business when she was just starting. But my own feeling, gleaned over many years of trying to respond to my own angel Enniss, is that the efforts of all these angels are coordinated through the one angel appointed to watch over us.

Another question is whether each of us has a different guardian angel. Neither scholars nor mystics have achieved any consensus on this point. It seems logical to me that one angel is certainly powerful and wise enough to watch over more than one individual. Perhaps a single angel takes charge of a whole family. (I remember a short-lived TV series called *Out of the Blue*, in which an angel comes into the life of three orphaned children and their aunt to be their guardian angel.) On the other hand, God is prodigal in love and care, and perhaps that extends to our angels, so that we each have a different angel.

For most of the history of the human race, the angels of God have worked largely in secret, only parting the curtain enough for us to be reassured of their presence and care. But in recent centuries, and most especially in our own time, things have changed—and that is the subject of the next chapter.

CHAPTER FOUR

WHY ARE THE ANGELS APPEARING SO OFTEN?

aybe their visits are a function of our own perceived need for spiritual help—and then again, maybe they're trying to tell us something wonderful.

When I speak of angels appearing, I mean much more than the personal encounters people are reporting so often, or even the "angels unawares" who help us in need. I mean the whole level of angel awareness, from the most mundane things like collections of angel statues to the most sublime words of angels that have come to us through human intermediaries. And most of all, I mean the increased awareness we have of the way angels are working in our lives and speaking to our hearts about the need to love, to live, to grow.

Almost every recent book on the subject of angels has speculated about why this is happening. The theories tend to fall into one of three areas: human realism, human troubles, human transformations.

Realism

Realism points out that in the history of the world, periods of intense materialism or concentration on things of this world are always followed by a similar swing of the pendulum toward the spiritual side of life. Selfish, me-first attitudes are succeeded by altruistic, philanthropic ones. The self-satisfied, complacent young people of the fifties are followed by energetic, spiritually hungry flower children of the sixties. And now a generation of men and women raised in the permissive, I-come-first era of the seventies and eighties are seeking the spiritual grounding they never knew during their formative years. And they are looking for it, not just in the established structures that have traditionally provided such nurture, but in alternative, new ways of looking at and seeking God and the purpose of life.

For both the orthodox believer and the New Age adept, the message and presence of the angels in our lives are important. Angels transcend every religion, every philosophy, every creed. In fact, angels have no religion, as we know it—their existence precedes every religious system that has ever existed on earth. An angel's creed is Love.

Spiritual hunger—the longing to know who we are and where we are going—is basic to our human nature. It can only be denied or rejected for so long before it must raise its head and cry out for recognition. If it is denied too long and too forcefully, either by society as a whole or in our individual lives, it rises up in persecutions and witch-hunts and other atrocities.

It is when we realize that there must be more to our lives than jobs and prestige and power and the accumulation of goods to no purpose that our angels are stepping in to help, to advise, to counsel. They have seen it all before—and they are working behind the scenes to restore the balance. It's as though, like any good public relations firm, they always know when to step in to trumpet their cause.

And what do they tell us? They want us to understand that heaven is not as far away as we think. The barrier between their dimension and ours can be bridged. We can see into heaven itself enough to give us hope that this dimension is not all there is. *God is not an old man sitting on a cloud who has forgotten you*, they remind us. *God is as near as your own heartbeat. You can grow, if you want to; you must grow. This world is not all there is.*

Troubles

Some say that angels are only noticeable when we're in trouble; when life is peaceful and calm they stay in the background.

It's certainly true that angels manifest themselves powerfully in people's lives when crises occur. Most of the people I have heard of or known personally who were touched by angels were at some crossroads or in some state of personal upheaval, whether grief or fear, or anxiety, or, paradoxically, joy or exaltation.

Skeptics say that our own need produces the angel. And it can be so at some times and in some places. But I am just as certain that a loving God, knowing our need, sends our angel to whisper to our heart that we are not alone.

We are in a period where people are increasingly afraid and stressed out by life. We feel depersonalized, made into numbers and statistics (I always found it significant that *numb* is a part of *number*). We have lost control over our environment, and we are fast losing control over our own lives. The media tell us what to like, what to wear, whom to believe, how to have safe sex, until our own inner voices sense that they are drowning. In 1992, the most sought-after alternative medical therapy in the United States was in relaxation techniques.

"Don't be afraid," the angels come to say. "We know a better way. May we help you understand it? Please let us help." I think that our angels are making themselves known as oases of peace in our lives.

Not only are we experiencing personal stresses, the world is in deeper trouble than ever. Global pollution, deforestation, depletion of the ozone layer, toxic waste, chemical and biological weapons, the threat of nuclear accidents or worse—these are all realities. Species are disappearing from this planet faster than we can even discover them. People are killed over the ownership of endangered trees that are the only source of an anticancer drug. More people have been killed by war, famine, and persecution in this century than existed on the whole planet when Jesus was born. Our technology has far outstripped our wisdom as a species. We are killing our future.

This is the only world we have. We cannot fly off to another planet once we have squeezed the juice out of this one. It has been given to us, not to dominate and rape, but to cherish and nurture, in trust for those who will come after us.

What we are doing to destroy the earth does not please the angels who work so hard to preserve it. Was the angel who watched over the passenger pigeon happy to see the death of the last of its kind, a whole species destroyed by the greed of the human race? Are they pleased by acid rain that destroys forests and sterilizes lakes? The angels helped to spin this world from the motes of dust that once circled a nascent sun. They know the development of life on this world better than we remember our own childhood. "No being has the right to destroy, to deface the face of God!" they cry.

"Let us help you transform it instead." The angels are in our midst in such power and grandeur to awaken us to the knowledge that everything in our world reflects the divine. All must be treasured. If a flower must be transformed into a healing medicine, then God's face is in the healing. But a flower transformed into a toxic waste dump reflects only the face of evil. "We can help you learn to treasure this world, as we do," the angels are saying.

Transformations

The angels' desire to teach us to grow and to become good stewards of this planet is one of the major reasons why people believe angels are making themselves known to us so frequently. This idea says that the angels are among us to help raise our consciousness, our spiritual awareness as a race, not just as individuals. It's almost as though the angels are here to give us a spiritual dose of a timed-release vitamin. This theory, which is generally couched in the language of the New Age, argues that the whole earth is hovering on the edge of a transformation so glorious that we have no idea how to describe it. The angels are among us as guides, to help us through and into a new level of consciousness on earth. And in time, we will come to see the angels who were all around us all the time and live with them as friends and helpers.

I believe that in a limited sense, this concept of transformation is true. I believe that angels are in our midst so that the world will be transformed. But I don't think they're planning to do the work themselves. Their more obvious presence in our lives is to wake us up to the need for *us* to begin transforming the world that we both love so much. And once we have grown so loving that we have changed ourselves and the world around us, we will hardly need help to see and walk with our angels. God only knows how long this will take. Sometimes it seems to me that the only brink we are on is the brink of disaster. I hope we have the wisdom to learn, and I know that is part of the reason the angels have become so visible recently.

Of course our angels want our personal transformation no less than that of the earth. And that's as it should be. We cannot change the world for the better if we cannot even change ourselves, and rid our lives of jealousy and envy and prejudice and greed and all manner of evils. And we cannot do that without the presence of God in our lives.

The angels in our midst are signposts of hope that our transformation—and that of the whole world—is possible. *Heaven is not a galaxy away,* they say; *it's here; the kingdom of God is here, in your very midst—and here we are to prove it. The barriers are not insuperable. Your problems are not insoluble. God is as near as your heartbeat.*

I certainly believe that God's angels are working for our transformation. Beginning in 1979 and continuing for three years, I received certain intuitions or heart-to-heart communications from my own guardian angel. He told me that about 250 years ago, many of the angels who are guardians to the human race entered into a new way of working with their wards in this world. I have always called it *The Pilot Program.* Since it started, an increasing number of angels have been "seeded" on earth. These angels and their human wards are covenanted together to live in a much closer and more obvious spiritual relationship than most humans do, in order to become a leaven among all, for the transformation of the world. The idea is not that a few privileged become an exclusive club, but that angel and human act as hubs or nuclei around the world, with the aim that in time, all people and their guardian angels will share such close relationships. There's nothing magical or superstitious about it. It's not a private pipeline to God. It's simply another means by which God bestows grace upon us.

I have been part of *The Pilot Program* since that time. I learned that when I was touched by my angel Enniss at the age of five, it was with such transformation in mind, to free me of the fears that would have paralyzed my life. And as I've grown over the years, I've come to know that God intends for all of us to live lives filled with love and holiness and wholeness, and our angels have a major role to play in helping us learn to do just that.

The stories that follow, as in my own story, show angels at work in the lives of different people, some religious, some not, some adult, some children. Sometimes the angel came in a glorious light, and sometimes carrying a briefcase. And the angels' missions ranged from saving lives to salving spirits.

I hope these stories will touch you as they have touched me.

Chapter Five

Angel on a Train

Robin Diettrick, Ann Arbor, Michigan

Some have entertained angels unawares.
—Letter to the Hebrews 13:2

Angels come to help and guide us in as many guises as there are people who need their assistance. Sometimes we see their ethereal, heavenly shadow, bright with light and radiance. Sometimes we only feel their nearness or hear their whisper. And sometimes they look no different from ourselves—until, their work done, they leave suddenly, quietly, with only a hint of halo or a wisp of wing behind to make us wonder. Robin's story is a beautiful example of an angel in disguise.

I have always felt that I saw my guardian angel when I was a young married woman. My husband, a career military man, had been sent to Germany, and after nearly six months there alone, he asked if I would be willing to

71

come to Germany with our three young children. I said yes, because I missed him as much as he missed me.

It took me nearly three months to make all the arrangements for our move overseas. I had planned to leave in early June after our oldest child had finished the school year in America. We felt that if she had the whole summer to get used to another country and way of life, it would be easier for her to adjust to a new school in the fall. And, since I am a teacher, I would also be finished for the summer. But juggling packing, garage sales, and renting out our small house, not to mention final exam time in the high school where I taught history, was an exhausting effort. Some nights, looking at the stack of boxes that my father-in-law was going to store for us, I wondered how I was going to make it.

Of course I also made an effort to learn a little German. A fellow teacher gave me pointers during lunch period when we did not have monitor duty. But I have never had much of an ear for foreign languages, and although I learned a few courtesy phrases, actually speaking was beyond me.

Finally the day came for our flight to Germany. It was emotionally draining, mostly on me, as I kissed my mother and two older brothers good-bye. I knew we would not see each other for perhaps two years, and phone calls would be infrequent. I was trying to hold back tears when the flight attendant came up to me to help me get the children boarded in advance.

I didn't enjoy anything of the flight. It would have been a hard trip with three children, two of them not even in school yet, in any case. But this night, not only was the plane late and the air turbulent, the kids got airsick. I spent half the flight taking them to the bathroom and cleaning them up. By the time we were across the Atlantic, I was queasy, too. Toward the end of the flight, they fell asleep for a while, exhausted, but I was too nervous to relax. Perhaps the fact that I had drunk enough coffee to float our 747 was the reason.

I gave a small sigh of relief when we arrived at the airport in Germany. I knew we would clear customs and that my husband would be waiting for us to take us to our new apartment. I pulled together our baggage—I had two heavy suitcases and three shoulder bags—and put the twins in the fold-up stroller I had purchased in advance of the trip, and headed out toward a sign past the customs area marked AUSGANG/SORTIE/EXIT. I thought with relief, *Now everything is fine. I just have to find Alex and we will be on our way.* It was even a bit fun, listening to the sounds of German all around me on the loudspeaker. Of course I didn't understand a word. I looked around, but I didn't see my husband. *Well,* I thought, *he's probably been delayed in traffic. We'll just wait by the exit and he'll come along.* So I found a conspicuous corner and sat down with the children, who fell asleep in minutes.

Meanwhile, I sat on our bags, waiting for my husband and feeling increasingly alone and nervous, especially since I didn't speak German at all. Time passed, a half hour, an hour, more. My oldest woke up and was cranky. I had to take the children to a restroom, and risked leaving our bags, since I was too tired to handle them, too.

Finally, I thought I ought to call the base, but as I looked at a bank of phones, very different from what I was used to in the States, I realized I had no idea how to work them, even though I knew the number of my husband's office at the base. The instructions were in German, and the few words I had learned did not include a single one on the phone instructions. My exhaustion and frustration all caught up with me. I was close to tears. *Oh God, what am I going to do?* I asked myself.

Then I heard a man's voice in my ear. In impeccable English, it said, "May I be of some small assistance, Madam?" I turned around and saw a middle-aged gentleman standing next to me. With great relief I explained that I didn't know how to make a phone call.

He was very kind as he took the phone number and put some change into the machine. I was embarrassed that I didn't have any German coins, but he just took out his own wallet with a smile.

Soon I was talking to a soldier at my husband's base. He said, "I'm so glad you've called. We didn't know how to get a message to you." He then went on to explain that my husband had had a small auto accident and was in the base hospital getting a broken ankle attended to. I was most upset at this, after the stressful plane trip and all, because I had no idea how to get to the base from the airport. It was a matter of at least two hours to the hospital where my husband was, and I had no idea about trains or buses or public transportation. A taxi or limousine was out of the question. As I hung up the phone, I started to cry; then I tried to stop because I didn't want to worry my children. I had to be strong for them. But the tears fell down my face anyway.

The gentleman patted me kindly on the shoulder. "Don't worry, Madam, I will show you how to get a train for the base," he said. And he reached into his briefcase and pulled out a thermos, poured me some coffee, and had me drink it, as though there were nothing in the whole world to be anxious about. He was really so calming, and I found myself just following him around to this counter and that, while in what sounded like flawless German he explained my situation and need. He was a very ordinary man in a very ordinary business suit, with an old-fashioned briefcase of tan leather that opened from the top. He wore a crisp hat like a fedora, with a tiny feather in the hat brim. I remember wondering if he was Austrian (I had watched a number of travelogues while I was preparing for the trip). There was nothing about him to make me think he was an angel. I just thought to myself, *What a really kind man! God bless him.*

Soon after that, he hailed a taxi for me, told the driver in German to take us to the train station, told me what the fare would be and how to pay it, and before I could say anything more, just walked quickly back into the terminal with a jolly wave of his hand. I was so grateful to him that I could have kissed him.

The ride to the train station was uneventful, and we all began to calm down a bit, but once we were deposited outside the large building, I knew I was lost again, and the feeling of exhaustion and panic set in once more. I had tickets, but I didn't know where to go or what to do. We went inside; it was just a big, impersonal train station, and I couldn't understand the signs. I felt like crying again, and this time the lump in my throat was harder to clear. I looked at the tickets and turned them over. And I saw, written on the back, in neat, European-style handwriting, the instructions to get to the proper train track. *God bless that man!* I said again to myself.

Soon we were all standing on a platform awaiting the train that would take us to where my husband's base was located. A train pulled in, and I started to get all our luggage, and, of course, the three children, aboard. It took several trips, and by the time I was finished collapsing the stroller, I felt like collapsing myself.

We had barely sat down, however, when I looked out the window, and there was the gentleman who had helped me with the phone and train tickets. I watched, astonished, as he calmly walked into the car and said, "Excuse me, but this is the wrong train you're on. Your train will arrive after this one leaves. This train is going elsewhere. You must get off right now." And he proceeded to pick up two heavy suitcases and three shoulder bags as if they were empty and started for the exit.

I remember I collected the children, who were very disoriented by now, and followed him as if I were in a daze. I wondered where he had come from. Had he followed us to the train station?

Together we waited for the right train. I had thanked him sincerely for his help and he had replied, "Quite all right, Madam, quite all right," but said little else. He wasn't unfriendly at all, just not the talkative sort.

When the train arrived, he settled me, the children, and our belongings in our seats and spoke to the conductor privately. "The conductor speaks some English, Madam," he said politely. "He will assist you at your destination."

And then, since the train was about to pull out, he waved a little, and headed toward the exit, which was in plain view. I opened the window and leaned out, so that I could thank him again once he was back on the platform.

But he never came out the exit! I had seen him open the door and leave the coach—and there was no other place for him to go. He just disappeared!

Absolutely astonished, I looked up and down the platform; then I went across the aisle and did the same. But there was no one around. The only people on the platform were white, and he had been black, like me and my family.

I sat back down as the train moved out of the station. The children fell asleep, exhausted, but I was too nervous to relax, even though the conductor had told me our stop was not for nearly two hours.

Eventually, however, I did sleep, and I slept deeply, for a long time. Then, suddenly, I heard a voice saying "Wake up! Wake up!" I think I only heard it in my mind or in my dream, but it was the voice of the helpful stranger, that I'm sure of. I sat up, but he wasn't there. However, the train was pulling into our station.

I roused the kids and, with the help of the conductor, got the baggage and all onto the platform. A young American soldier came up to me and said that my husband had asked him to meet me. I remember I just stood there and cried like my two-year-olds. The odyssey was over.

Later, at my husband's bedside, I told him my story. "He sure was a guardian angel to you and the kids," he said.

And you know, I believe he was right—literally. God knew we needed help after Alex broke his ankle, and sent His angel to guide us and keep us safe, until we could be reunited at the hospital. I really do believe that.

I didn't share my story with too many people, because I felt a little funny telling others about an angel in a fedora with a thermos full of coffee. But there's no doubt in my mind that he was an angel in human form. It was more than just his kindness and his helpfulness. It was the way he knew in advance my need for help, with the phone, the taxi, the train. It was the way he helped me without ever being intrusive. It was a really gentle kind of authority; he never ordered me to follow him or anything. I just felt safe and secure when he was helping us. And the way he disappeared into thin air after getting us on the right train is something I will never forget. I've never seen him again, of course, but ever since then I have been sure that my family has a guardian angel looking after us in whatever fashion angels watch over us.

I have consciously tried to imitate my angel in helping others in little things whenever I can, as my way of giving thanks to God for the help He sent me that day. I try to be a "secret angel" to others. It might mean an unsigned note to a fellow teacher praising his patience with a difficult student. Or it might mean leaving an envelope of coupons for dog food that I've clipped on the chair of a coworker who has two Irish wolfhounds. Or maybe I'll sit with a neighbor's children so she can run an unexpected errand. I just feel like I need to give something back for all the help I received that day. I know we're not angels, but we can be angels in a sense to those around us.

We returned to the States about two and a half years later, and I remember looking around the train station

and the airport, wondering if I would see my angel helping someone else. I didn't, but I have the feeling that he
is still there, maybe dressed as a flight attendant or as
another traveler. Maybe he looks like a woman; maybe
he's now white or Asian; maybe he's older or younger. I
hope he has touched other lives as he touched mine.

I will never forget him.

Chapter Six

The Angel of Healing

Caroline Sutherland,
Hansville, Washington

> At that very time, the prayer of these two suppliants was heard in the glorious presence of Almighty God. So Raphael was sent to heal them both.
> —Tobit 3:16

ngels bring healing into our lives, and when we need it, a sense of direction. They can help clarify in an instant our doubts and uncertainties, because they see the whole more surely than we do; they see with God's eyes, as it were. And when we let an angel touch our life to heal us, then we, too, can be instruments of spiritual healing for others, as Caroline is.

It always amazes me how much of our precious lives we can live on this planet without ever asking ourselves the most important question of all: Why am I here?

I know it was a question I hadn't asked myself when I

was young, so the Universe reached out and asked it for me and sent my angel to make sure I answered it. I've been trying to do just that for the past decade, and the more I meditate about the question, the more I am led to become the answer.

Nothing in my childhood led me to suspect I would ever become a means through which people might be healed of all manner of spiritual ills and fears, except perhaps that my father was a physician, so I saw people's need for healing in an immediate and powerful way. Because he was with the United Nations, we lived in many different places and countries as I was growing up. We belonged to the Anglican Church, and I always enjoyed going to church and singing in the choir (but I can't say I ever really thought about angels). In the summers I would go away to church camp, and I always felt very close to God when I was surrounded by nature. But I never had any spiritual experience there, either.

College was followed by a career as a free-lance newspaper and magazine writer. I married a business executive and set about raising two lovely daughters. I took them to church and to Sunday School and sat in the pews myself. On the surface, one would have thought that my life was almost perfect.

But under the surface, doubts and questions were already starting to form. A popular song of the period, "Is That All There Is?" might well have been my theme. By 1983, my unhappiness and dissatisfaction with my inner life was profound. I searched for answers, but I felt blocked. I called out to the Universe for the reason for my life, and I could not understand the reply. The Anglican Church that I had attended all my life did not help me understand why I was put on earth. And I could sense that my marriage was beginning to be in trouble, too.

And then I received a visit from an old friend whom I hadn't seen in years—and what she had to tell me and show me helped me focus my life.

When she came over to visit, I hadn't planned on sharing with her all of my doubts and uncertainties and my inability to see the purpose of my life. I knew that she had just gone through some devastating personal tragedies—her husband had recently deserted her and gone off with another woman. But instead of being upset or anxious, or angry or bitter, she was full of energy and vitality, and her peace and serenity and self-confidence were extraordinary. I couldn't believe that in the face of all she was going through she could be so calm. I knew that if such a thing happened to me, I would be a basket case.

"What's your secret?" I finally asked her.

She told me about some courses in the area of meditation that she had been taking recently, which, she said, had helped her immensely in becoming so focused and positive. I asked her if she could teach me something of what she had been learning, and she showed me some of the meditation and visualization techniques that she said had helped her. I had never experienced anything like them before, and from that moment I went on to study them in depth with the same teacher she was working with.

As I got deeper into meditation, I began to take more control over my life and to realize that my thoughts and actions were important, that I was here on earth for a reason that I had to find. Instead of being unfocused, my mind and my sense of purpose in life sharpened. I became aware of my inner guide, the "still, small voice" we all have, that comes from God, from the Universe, and that knows the truth about us. I began to pull the loose strands of my life together.

I've often wondered if I would have been able to see my angel had I not been prepared through serious meditation. Perhaps my angel had tried to guide me before, but I wasn't sensitive or focused enough to recognize it. Or perhaps my angel sent my friend to me that day, so that I could learn to sense my inner voice and become spiritually aware enough to recognize the angelic when it came into my life.

Once I had begun my spiritual journey, I could see more clearly the things in my life that were serious obstacles. I knew I would have to do some major house cleaning. One of the first things to go was my job at the newspaper. The more I looked at it, the more I knew it was not feeding my spirit—for me, it was a dead end. I could feel my inner voice telling me to let it go. So, even though I had nothing else to take its place, I gave in my notice in November of 1983. And so beautifully does the Universe orchestrate things, that a young woman I had been teaching something about my work was able to step right into my old job without missing a measure.

In the meanwhile, I made an appointment with my doctor, who had been treating me for food allergies and candida infections. He was a clinical ecologist, a specialist in environmental medicine, and deeply committed to a holistic approach that treats the whole person, not just a symptom or an illness. I told him I would be leaving my job at the paper, and he said it was a good move—that I would get rid of a lot of stress that way.

With the holidays over, I intensified my meditations, asking to be shown my life's purpose. I didn't address God specifically; I wasn't sure at that time that there was a God, at least not in the conventional sense I had grown up with. But I knew, of course, that there was some kind of a higher power, and I reached out to that with all my strength.

About three weeks later, my doctor called me up and asked me if I could come over and meet with him. And during the course of our meeting, he asked me if I would be his assistant in the clinic. I sensed the rightness of it—I had always been interested in medicine and healing, and I respected his approach to healing a great deal. My inner voice told me that this was my next step in life, and I started working in the clinic in June of 1984.

In June of the following year I spent a long weekend with the friend who had first taught me about meditation. She had called me and said, "Why don't you come on over and we'll spend some time together working on meditation and taking long walks in the country." What with my new job and the demands of my family, I really appreciated the opportunity to get away for a few days.

Over the course of the weekend, we talked and spent time in very intense meditations, mainly healing meditations. It was a very special time for me. My inner perceptions became very clear—I felt as though I were standing outside myself and looking in with great clarity, as though my mind or my spirit was wide awake and everything around me was going on in slow motion. I had a feeling of expectation, but I didn't know of what.

After three days with my girlfriend, I returned home and to my job at the clinic, but that heightened sense of perception persisted strongly. I felt as though I could see and hear beyond what I would see or hear in a normal sense of awareness. Thinking back on it, I can see that my angel was starting to prepare me for what was to come. I was in an extremely receptive state.

Several days later, I went into the clinic early to prepare the homeopathic medicines for the day's patients who started to arrive at eight in the morning. I always had a special connection to or affinity for these medicines; I had seen how they healed people; and I really enjoyed going in early to prepare them.

The clinic itself was small. My office was in front of the tiny reception area, with diagnostic equipment on one side and the table with the medicines we used on the other. At that time we were working with some special substances designed to help strengthen people's immune systems.

It was half past seven when I felt a tremendous energy in my heart, a quickening, a feeling of warmth and heat. This sensation was familiar to me; it usually preceded some type of awareness or understanding or intuition; sometimes just to be around the healing medicines itself produced such a sensation. I felt a presence, and I looked up, and it seemed to me as though the entire end of the room had opened up, and a light was growing in its place. The back wall, the floor, the ceiling—all faded away, to be replaced by the most incredibly beautiful light I have ever seen. I had the impression that the light had far more substance than the room, and had overlaid its reality onto that of the room, replacing it, for the moment, or that the room had become a tunnel, with its one end completely open to the light. The light was so intense I could hardly stand it, at first.

And standing there in the midst of the light appeared a very quivering, vibrating, pulsating being of light with outstretched wings that curved down a bit at the tips, as though they were reaching out to embrace me, and a face that was very loving. And although the figure itself shone with an intensely bright, vibrant, transparent white light, the wings and the head and the angel's face were colored like the northern lights, the aurora borealis. I saw such beautiful colors—pink, yellow, green, white, and gold, sparkling and vibrating. The light was very solid—I couldn't see anything behind it.

The angel herself was tall. The room was about eight feet from floor to ceiling, and I had the impression that the angel was taller; perhaps the body was about ten feet tall. Keep in mind that the end of the room had totally faded out. I got the impression that there was more of the angel than what I could see.

I felt such love reaching out toward me and all around me as I had never experienced before. I had the sensation of knowing that I was never alone, that this being was always with me in some way to comfort me. The face was full of compassion, loving, soft, and gentle. There was a tremendous love energy in the room, and I was filled with that mystical presence.

When I saw the angel, my heart began to pound. I was absolutely awestruck at the sight, but the sight of the angel's face, full of love and peace, kept me from being afraid. *Why me?* I thought. *Why should this be happening to me?*

"Behold the angel!" The words came to my mind as if the angel—or perhaps God or the Universe itself—had spoken. I believe she spoke in my heart—I did not hear any words aloud. "Will you do my work?"

For me, that question went to the heart of my being. I had been searching for years for the answer to it. What *was* my work? There was no doubt in my mind that I was seeing the "other side" and I would commit to whatever it was I was called to do. I also felt the angel was telling me that I should try to become as angel-like in my everyday life as I could, more aware at every single moment of how precious life is, more reverent in my relationship with the patients in the clinic.

Here I am! I communicated. *Whatever the work is, I am ready to do it.* And after I had answered, the angel and the light that surrounded her began to fade, and the room resumed its ordinary appearance. I'm sure that the entire encounter took only a few minutes or seconds, because the patients hadn't started to arrive, but I believe that in the moments when we encounter angels, we are drawn into their dimension to some extent, and our sense of time is altered.

After the vision faded, I was so full of light and energy that I just had to move around. I felt as if I had just been given a window, a gift that would stand me in fabulous, wonderful stead for the rest of my life. I was bathed in this energy, and I just had to move around and pinch myself. And my senses were heightened to a level I had never experienced. I remember putting my ear to some flowers—anthuriums—on the desk in the reception area, and I could hear music like sweet flutes and choirs from these flowers. It was an extraordinary experience.

And then I waited for the doctor and patients to arrive. All that day, I had the feeling that I was beginning my training in the work the angel had asked me to undertake, and I have felt that ever since.

The aftereffects of this vision were profound, certainly in terms of my relationship with other people. I began to have a lot more respect for those in my life—my children, my husband, the patients in the clinic. I began to understand the depth and magnitude of creation and the blessing that my life was. I came to understand that I had to change much in my attitude toward life and the people around me, that I needed to work intensely on a profound interior transformation in my life.

I also found that I had become very intuitive about the patients. Often, I knew what had to be done to make them well. I knew what organs were affected and how short or long their illness would last. I still have this great gift, and I still help the people who come to me for assistance, although I'm not currently employed in a clinic setting.

In 1986 I was led to leave the clinic and start my own practice in relaxation therapy. I had by this time completed various courses to enable me to teach people to relax. Several miracles led me to an adorable small office and many clients who would be the testing ground for the audio tapes that the angels would enable me to produce. During that powerful time my marriage ended, and how I helped my children over the initial challenges of that period is written in my book, *Mommy I Hurt*.

Although I never actually saw the angel again, I was given a vision on November 27, 1987, that led me to create an angel doll with audio tapes to reassure children that they are special, valued, and loved. I awoke early, and as I sat up in bed, meditating, my angel gave me the whole format for the angel doll and tape, which I later called *My Little Angel Tells Me I'm Special*. It was so vivid it was like looking at a ticker tape with the words printed right on it. I had a vision of children crying and rubbing their eyes and saying, "Help me, please help!" And I saw them receiving the angel dolls and listening to the tapes and having their fears and anxieties ease away.

I started the very same day to bring the vision to reality. While having lunch with a friend, I shared the vision with him and asked hesitantly, "Do you know anything about dolls?"

He looked at me incredulously and said, "Well, you know it's the funniest thing. I have this friend who told me recently that someone would come to me with an idea for a children's project."

That was the beginning; since then everything I've needed for the project has come to me. Of course there have been delays and log jams, but the angels have always overcome them.

The results have clearly shown that the project was inspired. I have so many letters in my files from parents whose children have been helped by the tape and the angel doll that I have no doubts on that score. There's no question in my mind that I should be doing this work. If I ever get to a point where I think, *Oh, my goodness, I'm getting frustrated or tired of this*, I always get an encouraging phone call or a letter.

I have never seen my angel as I did that day in the clinic when I accepted with all my heart the work that I was to do, but I know their presence and their guidance in my daily life, and I seek it out. Whenever I do a new tape, I always feel that my angels are beside me, inspiring me, giving me the words, helping me to structure and deliver it. When I give talks and workshops, I know they are with me, and I just turn everything over to them. I've even been given a gift for painting the angels, although I'm not a trained artist.

Personally, my mission, although indeed tremendously fulfilling in so many ways, has been a tremendous challenge. I have had to learn to walk by faith, not by sight. Every day I listen inside and the message is always to keep going and to have faith. And although I no longer have the financial and other kinds of security I once considered so important, I believe I have found the "pearl of great price"—inner security and trust.

Have I been touched by angels? Yes, without question, and I hope and expect it will continue all my life until I leave this dimension of earth and beyond.

Chapter Seven

The Angel Who Saved My Marriage

JAMES DIBELLO, *Phoenix, Arizona*

"I was sent from heaven to heal you."

—TOBIT

---

ometimes truth is stranger than fiction. I remember a Hollywood movie from the fifties, *Forever Darling*, that starred James Mason as a guardian angel who came to save Lucille Ball's marriage to Desi Arnaz. Jack diBello's story reminds us that angels come into our lives as much for the others in them as for ourselves.

My wife, Marie, and I celebrated our thirty-fifth wedding anniversary in 1992. We raised three children, all of whom have been real joys in our lives. They've gone on to have families of their own, so we now have six grandchildren here on earth, and one already waiting for us in heaven. And I don't think any of the blessings I have known would have happened if my guardian angel hadn't saved my marriage one strange and awful night.

I grew up in the Midwest in an intensely Catholic family, one of six children. My grandparents on my mother's side had come from the Abruzzi region of Italy to the United States. They lived with us, so we had a real full house at times.

In our house we believed in angels, I mean, we really *believed*. Sometimes my mother would joke that the angels were just as much family members as we were. One of the first prayers I ever learned to say, after the Our Father, was "Angel of God, my guardian dear, to whom God's love entrusts me here, ever this day be at my side, to lead and guard, to light and guide." When my two brothers and I said night prayers with Mama, we would always say it together, and change day to night.

I remember my Nonna—that's what we called our grandmother—would set an extra place at our already crowded dining room table on certain feasts and especially on our birthdays. That was for our guardian angel. On our birthdays we set the extra place ourselves. Nonna said that it was a way of showing respect, of thanking one's guardian angel for all he had done during the past year, and of asking his help in the year to come. And we'd all have to move over and make room, just in case our guardian angel showed up. And whenever we went to Mass as a family, Mama always told us to let our guardian angels into the pew first, again as a gesture of respect. (However, we didn't have to leave room for them to sit. I don't think the ushers would have been pleased if we had.)

In school, the nuns taught us about angels, too. We were forever drawing angels and doing angel crafts, and for the Christmas pageant one year, everyone in the third grade who didn't have another part got to dress up in white robes and be part of the heavenly choir. (I played a shepherd, so I wore burlap instead, and I itched.)

Such an ordinary childhood—for a while, anyway.

And then when I was fourteen my younger brother Frank began to be ill. He tired easily and he just hung around the house, and all he had to do was touch something for him to sport a new bruise. I didn't know it at the time, but Frank had leukemia, an acute type that often strikes children. In 1948 it was an automatic death sentence—even today, I believe a cure requires herculean measures.

Frank was my favorite brother; he looked up to me for some reason and always wanted to do what I did. I was a normal, often mischievous kid, and I got Frank in trouble with Mama on a fairly regular basis, but he never seemed to mind. I taught him how to ride my bike soon after he started becoming sick, hoping to cheer him up, but before long he couldn't even push the pedals.

I was not a particularly observant child. I never noticed the gloom that hung over our house as Frank became even more sick from the leukemia. He was in the hospital more often than not, and Nonna took care of us when our parents were with him.

And then one day they came home from the hospital

crying, but trying to be brave. The priest from our parish was with them. And we all gathered together with much solemnity while the pastor told us that Frank's angel had taken him to heaven to be with Jesus. We all cried and cried and asked questions of Mama, who was too broken up to answer, and of Nonna, who was so distraught she forgot most of her English and reverted back to Italian, of which I understood only a little.

At first, like everyone else, I was so sick at heart I just cried. But as soon as I had dried my tears for the moment, a slow and seething kind of anger began to grow in me, like a piece of metal turning gradually red, orange, yellow, and finally white hot. I felt as if I would explode.

Why hadn't my parents told me Frank was going to die? Why had they kept it hidden like some dark secret? *I never got a chance to say good-bye to him!* I screamed silently. And then, the ultimate question: How could the God I believed in have allowed it? Where was his angel? At fourteen, one is old enough to ask these questions.

Of course, my parents didn't tell me and my brothers and sisters when Frank's illness was first diagnosed because it just wasn't done back then. In fact, my parents never even told Frank he was going to die, although I'm sure he knew. When I saw him just before he died, he was so small in the big, white hospital bed with the blessed cross hanging on the wall. He had an IV in his arm and a big, clumsy oxygen mask on his face and an enormous, scary oxygen tank beside the bed.

Why did you let this happen, God? I asked, angrier than I had ever been in my life.

But God didn't answer me. It seemed as if all of the

94

childhood faith and trust I had had vanished as if in a nightmare.

I hate you, God! I screamed over and over again during the days and nights that followed Frank's death and funeral. And I hated Frank's angel, too. What a stupid thing to believe in. And the anger kept on growing, until I felt as if I wanted to punch the lights out of anyone and anything I saw.

They say that we all go through rebellious phases when we enter our teen years. I know I saw it with my own children. But with them, the rebellion seemed to come as they measured their own desires and wishes against mine and Marie's. They tested the limits we set for them, and when they mouthed off over some issue, we discussed it or argued it out, and we stayed close as a family.

The rebellion in my own young life, however, seems a lot different to me than what I've noticed in my own children or their friends. Frank's untimely death triggered an anger in me that I just couldn't control, a rage against anything that fell short of its goals or failed to achieve perfection, or was cut off before it could reach its peak. I had never heard the old saying "The moment of the rose and the moment of the yew tree are of equal duration," and I doubt I could have understood it, even if I had heard it. I became driven, even obsessed, with achieving all I could, doing everything I set out to do, and doing it as perfectly and as fast as I could.

When Frank died, I was in eighth grade at our parish school. Going into high school, however, meant leaving the hallowed halls of Catholic education and moving into the radically different world of our public high school. The difference is not so great today, but in 1950,

Catholic schools represented the epitome of strict scho-
lastic and moral education to many people. Our clothes,
our classes, our days, our activities were all planned for
us—there was very little room for individual differences.
To be thrown into the world of the public high school,
with hundreds of students from all over town; to have to
decide what to wear, what courses to take, what clubs to
join, was scary for most—and for me it was like being
thrown to the lions. I hated it, but by then I hated almost
everything and everyone.

My troubles had started at the funeral home the day
Frank was buried. I had been seething with rage all day,
but I had had no chance to talk to my parents. Finally,
at the end of the evening, after everyone had joined
together to pray the rosary, I just started crying hysteri-
cally from tension. And as my father reached out to hold
me or maybe even pat me on the back to break the
hysteria, I just reached out and landed a hard punch on
his jaw. Before he had even begun to show his shock, I
started screaming almost incoherently about Frank and
how my parents could have kept his illness from me. I
kept this up to such an extent that the funeral director
wanted to call a doctor.

My father recovered from the badly split lip I had given
him and the shiner, and no one made any attempt to
punish me, but my anger didn't go away. Over the summer between eighth-grade graduation and starting high
school, I punched out anything I could find. I lost my
best friend after beating him up because he hadn't paid
me back for the time I mowed his lawn for him. I stomped
all my mother's flowers into the ground. My father got
me a punching bag, thinking it would help—you know,

the kind on a metal stick, with a floorboard that you stand on to keep it stationary. I punched it out in a week.

When the fall came, I was a volcano waiting for a chance to explode. My parents had managed to deal with their grief at Frank's death and were just starting to realize I was in trouble. But my father was often away from home on business, and Nonna was just not the sort of person to be able to help me. Now, when she started to tell me about Jesus and the angels and heaven, I turned away. And when my birthday came later that fall, and I was supposed to set the table for my guardian angel, I threw the plate at the kitchen window, breaking both with a loud crash.

How I managed to get through high school, I still don't know. I've seen grown men far less driven than I was die of strokes. I went out for football and wrestling, and I blew off so much aggression in both sports that I lived on the edge of being kicked off the teams for violence, and being the best athlete on the teams out of sheer energy. At least, after a few lessons learned the hard way, I stopped picking on other students and daring them to fight me over trifles.

I had always been a good student, with something like a photographic memory and an especially keen ear for languages. Perhaps the latter came easily because I'd grown up with grandparents who spoke Italian as much as they spoke English. And I had had two years of Latin in parochial school. A school counselor, who seemed to understand my internal pain, always loaded me with the heaviest courses, which I was determined to succeed in. I read as compulsively as I practiced wrestling falls, and when I finally graduated from high school, I was third in a class of nearly five hundred (I hated the two students who were ahead of me). I had twelve letters in sports and the school award for excellence in Latin and German. I also had a scholarship to the state university.

And I still had my anger, although I was no longer throwing dishes through the windows. By now it had simmered down and was fueling my passion to be perfect in everything. I set myself impossible goals, and even when I succeeded, I paid a price. I remember the summer before I started at State, I had a sales job that paid on commission and virtually nothing else. In that one summer I made more on commissions than their top full-time salesman made in six months. How did I do it? I went out on leads seven days a week from morning to night, methodically, driven by the ever-present demon of anger inside.

It was toward the end of that summer I met Marie. She came to the door to hear my passionate spiel about the tools and gadgets I was selling, and as soon as I looked up into her pretty round face with her big brown eyes and freckles, I was in love. I never did anything in a half-a——ed fashion. I proposed to her on the spot.

Marie laughed, but I knew she wasn't laughing at me, just at the situation. Here I was on my knees, proposing, with a set of kitchen tools in one hand and socket wrenches in the other, and I don't remember if I had even told her my name.

And yet two years later, after my sophomore year at State, we were married. We were both barely twenty. Once I had seen my Marie, I never even looked at another woman. She was mine and I would have her—it was an attitude I was developing toward life in general.

It never occurred to me to ask her if she would mind being my possession.

For the next two years we lived with her mother— there was just no room at Mama and Dad's house—while I finished my degree in business with a minor in German. And for a while we were happy. Marie was working in a department store, and whenever I wasn't in class or studying, I still sold for the same company, although now I worked in an office. We were both trying to save as much money as quickly as possible so we could afford to buy a home of our own. Back in the fifties, it was a real possibility for a young couple. With my marriage and the distractions of school and a job, my anger had found a positive outlet.

After graduation, I was offered a very good job with an import-export business. Since one of their main lines came from Germany, my fluency in German came in handy. Soon they started dealing with a Japanese firm, and they sponsored me for a crash course in Japanese. By the time I was thirty, I was a vice-president of the firm, and Marie and I had a fine house and three children. She had wanted more, but I said no, which ended the matter, just as I expected.

My childhood anger had by this time reshaped itself into the hottest burning ambition to be seen anywhere. I found myself so totally enmeshed in business that often I wasn't home for days. I literally lived in my office, drinking stale coffee at two in the morning and washing my face at the water cooler. When I was at home, I was too tired to notice either my children or my wife. I had no friends, no social life, no outside interests. I lived and breathed the office, and at the time I truly believed I loved it. All that mattered to me were my own ambitions. I never even noticed that Marie and I were being forced apart by my obsessing over work.

Over the Easter weekend in 1969, my life came apart, unraveling with the speed of light. I was home, chafing at the bit, no work to do, no way to get into the office. It was evening, and the children were—somewhere. I never even noticed that Marie had not brought them home from Mass with her.

Marie came into the den, where I was working on some totally forgettable proposal, and said, without preamble, "Jack, I'm leaving you. I think I want a divorce."

I wasn't even listening to her. I started to say something like, "Come back soon," when I realized what she had said. I was so shocked I couldn't even speak.

Marie went on very solemnly to lay out what had been for her half a decade of married disaster with a husband who was either never home, or who was cold and calculating and who shut her out of his life entirely, and three children who scarcely knew who their father was. She pointed out all the times she had tried to get me to listen, and all the times I had turned her off.

"I've already taken the kids to Mother's, and I'm leaving to join them. It's up to you whether we come back." And she left, just like that.

For a while after she left, I just sat there. I, who was so glib and articulate in three languages, wheeling and dealing around the globe, couldn't even say boo to her.

And then something exploded within me. It was like my brother dying all over again, and once again I didn't know until it was too late. I went to the kitchen, looking for my usual anodyne—a bottle of Scotch. I got it out, set it on the table, and opened the cupboard to get a glass. Instead, I found myself systematically taking the glasses out and smashing them against the wall, the fridge, and the stove. Then I took out our good dishes and did the same. In minutes I was surrounded by broken crockery inches deep. Cans, bottles, utensils all went flying, while I raged. *How dare she mess with my plans? How could she do this to me? What is the president going to think at my company? How can I explain?* I thought as I looked for more things to break.

I reached the last cabinet in the kitchen. It held some old dishes my mother had given us years before. They were the ones we had used when I was a child, and they brought back memories of my brother that made me want to cry. I brought out the stack of plates, set them on the kitchen table, and threw them forcefully at the sink. But when I came to the last dish, I couldn't pick it up. I swear to God it stuck to the table. I tried with both hands to pry it up and I couldn't.

And then, while I stood there like a buffalo at bay, panting, sweating, my hands and face cut from flying glass and crockery, I heard a voice, a kind and compassionate voice that echoed all around me. And it said, "Jack, make room for me at the table. Jack, make room for me at the table."

I felt such a shiver of fear go through me I can't even begin to describe it. I let go the plate I was trying to wrestle off the table, and I looked down. I suddenly remembered Nonna saying, "Jack, make room for your guardian angel," and setting the table with an extra place. I remembered Frank's death and vowing I would never make room in my life for God or angels or anyone.

And I sat down on a chair and cried out my fear and hurt and anger until my head pounded and I couldn't cry anymore—for hours and hours.

Finally I got up to wash my face and blow my nose. Only then did I notice what I had done to our kitchen. It was a shambles. Every cabinet was empty, the fridge was empty. Pickle juice still dripped off the stove, and the floor was sticky with grape jelly. The pane in the door was broken. I had crushed one drinking glass by squeezing it, and my hand was badly cut. In fact, the dried blood had glued my fingers together.

But on the kitchen table, all by itself, free of the debris that covered everything, was that one old dinner plate. And as I looked at it, I heard the voice again, *Jack, make room for me at your table. Jack, make room for me at your table.*

I swear I heard this voice as well as I hear anything. It came from all directions, and it was the most beautiful voice, like an operatic soprano singing sweet Lieder.

"Who are you?" I gasped.

You know me, Jack, make room for me at your table. And the voice faded.

And I did know whose voice it was—it was my guardian angel's. I believe that for all those years she had been trying to speak to me, to reach me through all my anger and denial, but only when I had been brought to the end of my rope could she reach me. As distraught or as numb as I was, I knew the voice.

Without even thinking, I got up and brushed off the table. This time I picked up the plate without any problem, and set it at the end, where I usually sat. I retrieved a knife, fork, and spoon, and placed them around the plate, adding a napkin and an aluminum drinking glass that had survived my anger. Then I brushed off a chair and set it in place. I think I was saying, "Angel, please sit down; here, I'm making room for you."

I sat back in my own chair, just looking at the place setting, the only neat thing in the kitchen, and I felt the most incredible peace around me and filling me. I can't pretend I saw my angel across the table and that we had a spot of tea together. But I knew her presence, just as I had heard her speak to me. And I bowed my head and prayed the prayer I had learned as a child: "Angel of God, my guardian dear . . . "

When I had finished, I just started talking aloud to my angel about all the things that had been going on in my life, and most of all about Marie's leaving and taking the kids with her. I talked for a good hour without stopping. And I had the most extraordinary feeling that my guardian angel was right there, sitting across the table from me, even though I couldn't see her. And I felt that she was telling me, not just that I needed to change—I knew that—but that I could change, that the anger was gone that had skewed so much of my life.

The sky was just beginning to turn gray when I heard the sound of a key in the lock. It was my Marie. She pushed the door open, and as it opened, the sound of broken glass grated across the kitchen floor. She looked at me and at the kitchen, horrified; then she came across the room and threw her arms around me, and we both cried. "I couldn't sleep," she said. "Finally, it was like I heard a voice saying, 'Jack needs you, Marie.' It just kept repeating softly, over and over again. So I came."

I was so drained I felt like a little child again, needing

to be led rather than to lead. Marie took me out of the kitchen and into the bathroom, where she washed my hands and bandaged the one that was badly cut. She put me to bed without saying another word, and I slept like a baby until nearly noon.

After I woke, I felt disoriented, as though I had had the worst nightmare of my life. Then I saw my hands, all cut up, and everything that had happened came back in a rush. I jumped up and went to look at the war zone that had been my kitchen. It was as neat as a pin, except for all the scratches and dents and broken windows. Marie, looking tired but at peace, smiled. "I would never have believed this mess if I hadn't seen it with my own eyes. It took me hours to clean it up. It filled bags and bags of trash."

I started to apologize, but she shook her head. "We'll talk later, Jack. Just tell me one thing—why did you break up everything in the kitchen and then go to the trouble of setting the table?"

She pointed, and I saw that the old plate and the aluminum glass were still where I had left them after my guardian angel had asked me to let her into my life again.

"Marie, I have to tell you what happened," I said.

When I had finished telling her, she looked thoughtful. "You do seem different somehow, Jack. The tension is gone; you seem relaxed in a way I've never seen."

"Marie, I hope this doesn't seem silly, but I want to keep that place setting on the table forever. I don't ever want to take it off. If my angel hadn't come to me last night, I don't know what I would have done. I was in such despair I think I would have taken one of the carving knives and killed myself. I want to thank her and keep reminding myself of something I knew when I was a kid and then forgot."

"I think we can arrange that," she smiled.

That strange night was more than twenty years ago, but its effects have stayed with me ever since. I took a short leave from my job—God knows I had enough vacation time accumulated for ten people—and Marie and I went away on a cruise to Alaska for the first vacation we had had together since our honeymoon. We talked and talked, and I found all my old priorities changing for the better. With the help of God, Marie and I rebuilt our relationship on love and caring, not on anger and a compulsion to control. Ultimately, I left the company I had worked for since my college days—I just didn't want or need the stress anymore—and opened my own business working out of our home. I'm still a man who likes to work hard, but there's pleasure in it for me, not the sour fruit of anger and alienation.

And the old plate and the dented aluminum glass, the silverware and the napkin are still on our table, more than two decades later. They're my pledge to my guardian angel, and to God who sent her, that I will always welcome them at my table.

Chapter Eight
Walking with Angels

Martha Powers,
Columbia, South Carolina

Last night an angel of the God whom I serve came to me... —Acts 27:23

Some people keep the fact that they have been touched by angels a close secret, meant for them alone. Others, however, feel the need to speak out publicly about their experiences and to share them with others in many ways. Martha's story of how she came to start an angel-related business is most unusual.

I have felt my angels around me for my whole life, supporting me, protecting me, and inspiring me. Some of my most vivid memories as a child are of God's angels coming to be with me, to heal me, and even to play with me. And even though I don't see them now the way I did as a child, I still feel their love and their direct help, inspiring me to make their work better known to the world.

I was one of twelve children growing up in the South in the early forties. Our family farmed an area in rural South Carolina. I learned how to hoe cotton at an early age and to do all those chores that are part of the life of any farm child.

We were Bible-believing Protestant Christians. I remember my mother went to church just about any time the doors were open. She used to read the Bible a lot, and I still do, to this day. It's a very important book to me; I believe it.

I first saw my angels when I was five years old. At that time I had been hit by a car and critically injured. My worst injury was a bad depressed skull fracture—I had two or three real holes in my head, and I was in a coma for some three weeks. The doctors told my parents they didn't believe I was going to make it.

But I hung on, and when I finally woke up, that's when I first saw my angels. I was afraid, coming to in a strange bed and a strange room, but they came to me and told me not to be afraid, that I was going to get better. After I came out of the coma and was starting to recover, that's when the angels first came to my hospital room to play with me. I couldn't get out of bed, but I could see them clearly and touch them, and it seemed to me that in spirit we went for walks in the clouds. They kept me company during my long convalescence.

What I remember most about them is the speed with which they moved; they were very quick. They seemed to be able to go anywhere in just a twinkling. And in appearance they were almost transparent and light and fragile-looking, like a soap bubble. And they were very bright, with long, wavy hair. Sometimes there were as many as a dozen; sometimes I saw only two or three. I don't think I really thought too much about it; at that age one tends to accept things more or less uncritically.

From that time on, long after I recovered and resumed my normal life, I would play with the angels. And as I grew up, I began to experience their presence and their help in many ways.

I remember attending a Bible school when I was in second grade. We were supposed to come home right after the class was finished, because our mother didn't want us to walk home alone. It was a long walk, more than a mile and a half, and the back road was dangerous. But I often wanted to stay late, because the Bible school had different craft projects that interested me. So I would ask God to have my angels walk home with me—I would feel them beside me—and I wouldn't be afraid.

I became accustomed to asking my angels for all sorts of help, and they never failed me. When I was about twelve, I wanted very much to go to the summer Bible school at our church. It was about the beginning of June. But it was also a very busy time on the farm, and the cotton needed to be hoed, my father said. I asked and pleaded with him to let me go to Bible school, but he said the cotton had to be hoed and that was that.

Well, I went upstairs to my bedroom the night before and I got down on my knees and asked God for the angels to make it possible for me to go to the Bible school. "Just let it rain in the morning, just long enough so I can go to Bible school, then let it stop and I'll hoe cotton all afternoon," I promised my angels.

The next morning, early, we listened to the weather report. According to the announcer there was no rain in the forecast. But I prayed and prayed, and just before it would have been time to leave for Bible school, it suddenly started to rain; and it rained and it rained and it rained. We couldn't hoe the cotton in the rain, so Mother let me go off to Bible school.

We returned home about noon, and by that time the sky had cleared, and it looked as if it would be a beautiful day. I spent the afternoon hoeing cotton, as I had promised my angels.

The next morning, my father said that since the weather was supposed to be clear, we would not be able to go back to Bible school. "There's too much work to do here," he said. I ran back up to my bedroom to my favorite spot, got down on my knees, and I again prayed to God to have the angels make it rain "just enough for me to be able to go to Bible school." And within ten minutes I heard thunder and it started to rain again. So we got to go to Bible school the second day. The same pattern repeated itself all week.

Thursday night I remember the weatherman saying that the weather had been really crazy all that week, with freak little storms over very limited areas, when the overall weather indicated no rain in sight. But he announced that for the next two days at least the weather was sure to be clear. So Father once more announced we would be hoeing cotton the next morning; then he went up to bed. I decided I had better start praying right away, and I was sure the angels would once more cause it to rain.

But when I got up the sky was clear and the sun was shining. Still, I got dressed for Bible school. But Mother told me to go upstairs and change to some work clothes.

I got down on my knees again, and I started to pray. I was pretty angry at the angels. "You've just *got* to make it rain," I told them. "Today's the day we're having a party at Bible school, and you can't cheat me out of that. Besides, how will I be able to finish my projects that I've started?"

And then, just as suddenly as the sun had shone, the sky clouded over; and the next thing I knew, it was raining, just a little, but enough so my parents let us go to Bible school. And when we came back at noon, it was clear, and we went back to the fields to work. So the angels helped me after all to go to Bible school that summer—and the cotton was hoed, too.

I came to really depend on my angels to help me. I was like my mother in that I really enjoyed going to church, but it wasn't always easy. My father worked the third shift in a cotton mill, so he had to go to bed in the afternoon. That meant he couldn't drive us to church to the evening service. It was a mile and a half, and Mother wouldn't let us walk that road by ourselves in the dark; so I couldn't go to the service unless I had a ride. The problem was that we didn't have a telephone at the time, so I couldn't call any of our neighbors who were members of the church.

Well, I went upstairs and prayed to God for my angels to send someone by and pick me up—and then I got dressed for church and waited. My sisters said I was crazy, and they warned me not to come downstairs dressed in my Sunday best.

"Well, you better get dressed, too, if you want to come with me," I retorted.

"Oh, you're crazy; there's no one going to come and pick you up," they replied.

"Yes, there is; I prayed to God to have my angel send someone," I answered. Sure enough, at a quarter to six a car came up the long road leading to our house. "Just driving by and thought we'd stop to see if anyone wanted to go to church," our neighbors said. And since I was ready to leave, I did.

This happened more than once. Anytime I needed to go to church, it seemed that my angels would arrange for a ride.

All the time I was growing up and after I married and began raising a family, I always prayed to my angels when I needed help of any kind, and I always sensed they were near. Sometimes they helped me even when I didn't know I needed it.

I remember one night I was asleep in bed. My son Michael, who was just twelve at the time, was away at a Boy Scout overnight camp nearly twenty miles away. Suddenly, my guardian angel woke me up with a start and said to me, "Mike needs you!" It was about half past two in the morning. I sat straight up in bed, and I could still hear the words that had jarred me out of my sleep. "What's wrong?" I asked. And I could hear my guardian angel say, "He's cold and he's sick."

So I got up and put on my clothes and my coat and drove the long way to the campsite. It had started to rain and it was cold and wet. When I arrived at the campsite I found Michael; and he was indeed cold and wet and shivering. The boys' clothes had gotten soaked while they were putting up their tents in the rain. But what was worse, he had come down with a bad case of the mumps, and he was all swollen up in the throat. He really did need to come home, where he could put on dry clothes and get into a warm bed. He was very sick with the mumps, but I know he would have been much sicker if my angel hadn't woken me up to go and get him out of the cold and the rain.

As my children grew up, I found that my angels would help keep me informed about what they were doing. I know people will talk about this being just a mother's instinct, but it was more than that. I would actually hear my angels' voices telling me about things my sons had or hadn't done. I have three angels that I know about, besides the angels who, I believe, are assigned to the beginning of things, like my business.

I have found that it's very important to call on your angels. They can't help you as much as they would like to if you don't call on them. We all fall short sometimes by not asking their help. Angels are here to help us with the things we can't do for ourselves. I mean supernatural things, not the ordinary things. For example, a lot of people say things like, "Well, I posted an angel outside my door to guard my home, so I never worry about locking it up when I leave." But that's not really an angel's responsibility. You're supposed to take care of protecting your worldly goods yourself.

It really pleases angels when they can help us. That's their mission, and the more we let them do it, the happier they are. They love to do things to help us.

Once my children grew up, my life took a different turn. I began a jewelry business called Angel World, with guardian-angel pins to remind people of their own angels.

And the way the business began and has been guided has been a very special work of the angels in my life.

It all started back in 1976.

One night, it was about three in the morning, I was awakened by a hand shaking my shoulder. I turned over to go back to sleep, when a rush of adrenaline hit my system and woke me up totally. I had so much energy all of a sudden that I couldn't stay in bed. I got up and began to pace the floor. Then I sat down and read my Bible for half an hour, and then I sat quietly and prayed.

And then I noticed a pad and pencil on the desk. Without even thinking, I picked up the pencil and began to draw angels. Then, when I had finished the drawings, I felt tired again and I went to bed and slept until morning.

When I got up, I looked at the sketches and thought to myself, *I never knew I could draw like that.* So I sat down to draw more, and I couldn't, I just made a mess.

I put the drawings I had done in the night into a file, and didn't think much of them. But about three months later, the same thing happened—the same rush of energy in the middle of the night, the same urge to sketch angels and the accompanying talent to do so that I didn't have during the day. And this went on for about a year. I didn't know quite what to make of the drawings; I certainly had no idea of making jewelry with them.

During this time I had received a gold chain, the first one I ever owned, and I wanted to find a little gold angel to hang from the chain. But try as I might, there was just nothing available. I even got some wholesale jewelers I knew to check for me, because they went to all the big gift shows all across the country. And they all told me, "Sorry, there's just nothing out there."

Everything came together one morning as I was meditating. I was thinking about the drawings, and I happened to notice my gold chain lying on my dresser, and all of a sudden the flash bulbs went off and I knew why I had been given the drawings.

With the help of my angels I began the long process to have my drawings turned into jewelry. I copyrighted the designs and explored how to have the molds and models made. This took some years and many thousands of dollars.

One day I was getting ready to send the metal models to the manufacturer to have the three designs I had chosen made up. And that was the day my pocketbook was stolen. In it were the models, all my file information, the names and addresses of the people who were going to handle the modeling—everything. This was in October of 1986.

I was discouraged, to say the least. There was no way I could have afforded to have the models and all redone. So, after reporting it to the police, I tried to let it go. Nonetheless, I still felt the need to save as much money as I could, as one would do when starting a new business. I worked seven days a week, and was able to put a sizable sum away—but I didn't know for what.

And then one day some three years later—it was after Hurricane Hugo in 1989—I got a package in the mail. It was from a man who worked for the electric company. He had been out in a swamp in a nearby town trying to restore power, when his foot slipped on something in the mud. It was my purse that had been stolen years before!

His note said that the only things that were salvageable were my angel models, my keys, and my personal address book. And in that address book, the only entries that were still legible were my own and that of the manufacturer to whom I had been planning to send the angel models for reproduction. Almost three years had gone by, and I had given up the idea of the angel jewelry, but when the angel models came back, I knew I had to do it. And in my bank account was all the money I had been saving without knowing why.

I called the manufacturer and arranged for a thousand angels of each of the three designs to be made, in sterling and pewter and gold-plate. So now I had a huge inventory of angels that I needed to get out to gift stores.

My angels really helped me here. The largest gift show was the Christmas Show in Charlotte, but the waiting list of crafters, designers, and manufacturers was 420 deep. I was told that in five years or so I might be able to exhibit. So I went home, but I came back the next day—it was a two-hour drive—just in case someone might have canceled. But the woman I spoke to told me that even if someone canceled, they would still go down the waiting list. So I went home, disappointed. But the next day I found myself in the car again, heading for Charlotte. Once again I was told there would be no room and went home. And on the third day that same impulse from my angels made me make the long drive into the city. All the way in I was telling myself this was crazy, this was dumb, I was just wasting my time and gas—but I kept on driving.

When I got to the show, the woman who had told me I couldn't get in to exhibit was gone. In her place was another woman. She asked if she could help me, so I gave her a little brochure about my work.

"Oh, angel jewelry!" she said. "I've never heard of it before. Well, let me see." She pulled out a plan of the exhibits and looked at it intensely. "We really are all full up," she said, and my heart began to sink a bit, "but maybe I can make you a spot."

So she found me a little space at the end of the show, last in a list of more than three thousand exhibitors, and I set up my angel jewelry on the fifth day of the show.

I knew nothing about retail sales at that time. My display was almost nothing in comparison to the fine booths that the experienced exhibitors had set up. And I was at the far end of everything. But the angels brought people to my booth, and by the end of the show I had sold thousands and thousands of dollars worth of angels. Angel World was born that day.

Since then my business has grown, with the help of the angels. I know it has been with their help because of the response I have received from people who wear my angels. They write to me to say that wearing my angels reminds them of their guardian angel's love for them—and that's really what it's for.

I'm so happy that my angel jewelry reminds people of their guardian angel's love for them. I believe that God assigns an angel to each of us, with three responsibilities, and the major one is love. An angel loves you and loves you and loves you. The second responsibility is to protect your life and soul. And the third is to do for you the supernatural things you can't do for yourself.

This has become my mission in life—to promote the angels and their mission to help us.

Chapter Nine

Stormy Weather

Margaret Ann Gutierrez,
Roanoke, Virginia

The angel of the Lord encamps around those who revere Him and delivers them.

—Psalm 34:7

Many people are familiar with the classic picture of the guardian angel carefully shepherding a boy and girl across a small footbridge whose planks are falling apart. Sometimes this image is repeated in our own lives when we are touched by angels, as Margaret Ann can give witness to. Today Margaret Ann is a wife, a mother of two, and manager of a large department for a national corporation. But some thirty-one years ago she was just a frightened child in a thunderstorm.

Summers in upstate New York are short—the end of June, July, August, and then they're finished. Like any child, I enjoyed those times: playing with friends, swimming, picking berries in the woods. But of all the summers

117

of my girlhood, the one I remember most vividly is the one when my guardian angel came to lead me out of danger and into safe haven.

I was tall for my age, even when I was a child just starting school, and I was shy. As an adult, I can see that the family I grew up in was unusual. Perhaps it contributed to why I believe in angels. My mother was of Hungarian and German ancestry, born in Romania. My father was born in Brooklyn—his father was a Colombian, who was studying to be a doctor at Columbia University, and his mother an independent woman who pursued higher education and a career outside the home at a time when it was most uncommon. My mother was a laboratory technician, and my father was an English teacher at a nearby high school, who also coached sports. He ultimately became superintendent of schools in the area where we lived.

My father was also a yachtsman. He loved to sail and to race yachts. He had his own boat at a nearby yacht club, and he spent as much time as he could on the water. He knew about the clouds and the weather, the dangers of wind and waves to the yachts he loved so much, and how to interpret the signs in the skies. He always saw the importance of looking ahead, thinking quickly, and making sound decisions. Perhaps that's why he felt the need to call me the day my guardian angel touched my life.

I remember it was a Saturday morning. The weather was hot and muggy, with the threat of rain or a storm hanging in the skies overhead. I can still recall what I was wearing—blue shorts and a white T-shirt.

Because of the threat of storms, my father was home, rather than out on his yacht that day. He and my uncle were in the family room, huddled over a chessboard. My mother was working that day.

"Dad, I'm going over to Joanie's house to play with her and Nancy and Muffin," I told him as I headed for the door.

"That's fine; just be home in time for lunch."

So I went out through the back door and headed for my friend's home. It's important to the story to explain the geography of my neighborhood: Joan lived in the house almost behind mine; our backyards were separated by a small belt of trees and bushes. The easiest way by far to get to her house was to take a shortcut through our next-door neighbor's backyard—it was much easier than trying to force a way through the brambles and hedges at the back of our yard.

My parents weren't all that happy when I took this route, because our next-door neighbors had a large, rectangular, in-ground swimming pool, and the yard was not fenced in. At that time not all town ordinances required pools to be fenced. I think my parents were afraid that I might get too close and trip and fall in, and given the distance between the houses, if I cried for help I might not have been heard.

I, on the other hand, knew I was perfectly capable of taking care of myself; I was certainly not going to fall in my neighbor's pool. What was I, a baby? Besides, the regular route to Joan's house involved going all the way around the block, a long, long way. Everybody knows that the shortest distance between two points is a straight line, so that's the way I always took. Besides, our next-door neighbors didn't seem to mind.

So, taking my preferred shortcut, I set out for Joan's house. What with her brothers and sisters and friends, there was a sizable group of us who spent the morning playing games.

It was probably a good thing I had gone over to Joan's when I did. After I got there a bad thunderstorm broke out. The rain was heavy, and the winds strong. Thunder rattled the windows in Joan's house, and lightning lit up the leaden sky. But we played on, oblivious to the storm, having the Saturday morning fun that only children can have.

Just about noon my father called Joan's mother to have me come home for lunch. (I wasn't looking forward to my father's idea of cooking.) She called me to the phone.

"Yes, Daddy?" I asked.

"Margaret Ann, it's time for lunch."

"All right, I'm coming."

"Listen, I don't want you to take the shortcut home this time."

"But why not, Daddy? It's raining so hard, and if I take the long way I'll get all wet."

"The reason I want you to take the long way is so you won't have to go through the woods or past the Stillwells' swimming pool. This is a really bad storm, with lots of lightning, and lightning often hits water and trees. It will be much safer if you take the long way. You can always change your clothes before lunch."

"Oh, all right, Daddy," I said grumpily, looking out at the storm and watching the lightning streak the sky all around. I knew what he meant. I had been raised near a lake, where my father raced his yachts and my mother's family had a cottage, so I understood about the dangers of lightning.

I hung up the phone and told Joan's mother I had to go home for lunch. I thought I would go out the front door, but the idea of taking the long way around the whole block in the driving rain didn't appeal to me. *If I take the shortcut, I'll be all right,* I think I thought. *The lightning isn't going to hit me—I'm a big girl.*

I felt a little guilty about disobeying my father, but I was somewhat nervous about going out into the storm. I think I decided it would be better to spend as little time as possible under that threatening sky.

I left the house via the back door and was immediately pelted with large, cold raindrops. The sound of the thunder was louder outside, and the contrast of the strong forks of lightning against the gloomy sky made me feel more nervous.

I ran across the backyard of Joan's house as quickly as I could, and I slipped through the bushes that bordered the property. Now the belt of trees loomed ahead. Flashes of lightning lit up the trees, and my fear increased. *What if Daddy was right?* I thought. *What if a bolt of lightning really did hit?*

I thought of going back, but the way seemed especially long, and I could see our house. It seemed so close. I decided I would just run past the Stillwell's pool as quickly as I could. I dashed through the trees, feeling the ground rumble under my feet, and then I was through them and into an uncultivated area with tall grass and briar bushes.

I tore through that area and onto the manicured grass that made up the Stillwell's backyard. I took off running to get past the pool, which was on my left.

Just as I reached the midpoint, all hell broke loose in the skies over my head. A thunderclap that shook my teeth broke over me and lightning seemed to reach nearer the ground—and nearer to where I stood, exposed and vulnerable, at poolside. I wasn't a brave kid to begin with, and I cowered in fear, rooted to the spot, unable to move a muscle or to go forward or back. At this point the walkway beside the pool was narrow, and I couldn't move any farther to the right away from the pool. I knew I should have listened to my father, and I was positive that the next lightning flash would spear me like a fish, but I still couldn't move. I was paralyzed, as though a powerful hand was holding me back. Another strong thunderclap just in front of me was followed by lightning, which I feel might well have hit me if I had kept on running.

A flash of lightning to my right, over the belt of trees, attracted my glance. And that's when I saw my guardian angel.

She was standing just a few feet from me, the most exquisite, holy, beautiful being I have ever seen. To this day, the image has remained vivid in my mind. She was surrounded with a blue-white light, brighter than the lightning, that glistened and shimmered in spite of the storm. She had a beautiful complexion, and her thick hair was long and golden and wavy, and her eyes were a vivid blue. Around her forehead was a golden circlet like a headband.

I remember that the wonderful white light obscured

the lower half of her body so that I couldn't see her legs or feet. I just remember the upper part of her body. She was very tall.

The sight of my angel cut into my fear as a hot knife cuts into butter. Her face was so peaceful, so quiet and confident, and I felt some of that peacefulness come into me.

Time seemed to stand still while I stood there; at first I was a little taken aback and stunned, even apart from my fear of the storm; and then she spoke with me. I don't remember the exact words anymore, but I know she told me not to be afraid, to be calm, that I wasn't paralyzed anymore—I could walk away from the pool. And meanwhile the storm thundered and the lightning crashed all around me.

I found that my legs worked once more, and I wasn't trembling in fear. Suddenly I felt very peaceful and safe. It's a feeling that you never forget. I began to walk toward the front of the pool and the back of my neighbor's home. Once I had left their backyard, I could cut across to our backyard next door. And every step I took, my angel went with me, as if to encourage me, to let me know that she was watching over me. All of my fears of being struck down by the lightning went away, and I began to run toward my home. For most of that time my guardian angel kept up with me. Only when I had reached the safety of my backyard did I notice that she had vanished.

I ran into the house crying, "Daddy, Daddy! I just saw my guardian angel!" He was sitting cross-legged on the floor with my uncle, poring over the chessboard, and he looked up at me with a surprised expression.

Then he got up and went toward the kitchen. "You'd

better get some dry clothes on," he said. "I'll make you some lunch."

I changed and came back to the kitchen, where my worst fears about my father's cooking skills were confirmed. He had fixed me a cold hot dog. But I was so grateful to be sitting there safe and sound that I didn't mind.

When Mother came home, I told her I had seen my guardian angel; she still remembers my telling her the story. But as time went on, I never did share it with too many people—just members of my family.

I have often wondered why my life was touched by my guardian angel. I know that her first reason for appearing to me was to save me from the storm. It was so violent, with so much lightning, that I truly believe I would have been struck if I had stayed where I was. But even more, I've come to have a real sense of security about my life— that my guardian angel is watching over me to keep me out of harm's way. Other bad situations have happened to me, even bad automobile accidents, and in them all I've just had a quiet sense of confidence in the protecting power of my angel.

I really do believe in angels, because my life has been touched by their presence.

Chapter Ten

Angel with a Paintbrush

Andy Lakey, Murrieta, California

And Bezalel the artist...whom the Lord had
endowed with skill and understanding...made two
cherubim of beaten gold...with their wings
spread out.   —Exodus 36, passim

any people who have near-death
experiences report that they encountered angels while in that state. But
Andy's life was changed more than
most. As a result of being touched by
angels, he gained a new life, new
faith, even a new career.

Sometimes I think that my life—my real life—didn't
begin until the day I saw my angel on New Year's Day of
1986; that so much of what had gone on before in my
life was just dissolved into mist, and out of that mist
came the real Andy Lakey. Or perhaps it was as though

125

the angel had run a spatula across the still-wet canvas of my life, blurring all the old images and colors, and then began to paint with new, bright, well-defined images and colors on the former surface. In any case, the last few years of my life have been filled with a joy, a happiness, a peace, and sense of purpose I never knew before I saw my angel. I am not the same man I was before my angel touched my life.

What happens to people who have near-death experiences? It's not an uncommon event, from everything I've heard. Whatever brings one to the point of death, whether an illness or an accident, a near-death experience is powerful. In my case, as my spirit hovered between the earthly plane and the heavenly, I sensed the presence of my angel. It's always been hard to describe what I experienced that day, because our senses work differently when we are in between heaven and earth. I don't know if I saw my angel in the same way as I see things around me today. I'm not sure I heard my angel in the same way as I hear music and the sound of my baby daughter laughing. But something in me saw and heard—and remembered.

What did I experience? I felt my angel reach out to me and wrap his (or maybe her or its) arms around me in a gesture that was so protective and loving and caring and understanding I have no words to describe it. And whether or not I actually heard words, my angel communicated to me that I was going to be all right. I felt such reassurance and peace, and I understood that I was in the care of a loving God who had sent the angel as a sign of that love. The immense strength of that angel flowed through me, healing me, restoring me to life. I can't possibly convey what it was like to share in the life energy, the personal strength of the angel. And then the experience softly dissolved, and my spirit was reunited with my body.

I don't know how long the experience lasted, or whether it took any time at all. I don't think time has any relevance on the other side. But in whatever time or timelessness it took for that angel to wrap its arms around me, something deep in my heart changed for the better and forever. When my consciousness was restored, I was different, and I knew I was different.

I remember waking up, and my vision—as well as my insight—was sharper than it had ever been. I looked back at the first twenty-seven years of my life, and I saw how much I had wasted and ruined. And I think the realization would have been totally devastating if it had not been for the sense of utter peace that my angel had left with me as a sign of God's love for me. Not only did I see the need for a complete change in my life, I felt empowered to make those changes, because the strength of my angel was with me, too. I knew that with God's help and the support of my family, I could—and would— try to give back something to God in thanks for my life having been given back to me. And I had a sense that my future was going to be wonderful; I didn't know in what way.

In retrospect, I can see that this was not the first time I had known the help of my angel. There were incidents from my childhood that I can see were stamped with an angelic presence. I remember as a young child playing with my father on the front lawn under the tree. Suddenly, my mother tells me, I simply got up and ran for the front door, for no apparent reason. My father, who had been sitting on the ground, started to crawl after me, thinking, perhaps, that I was still playing a game. Just as he moved away from the area where we had been playing, a squeal of tires in the distance was followed by a car of drunken teenagers out of control, who smashed into the tree where we had been playing. Had I not run for the house, with my father following after, we both would have been killed. Coincidence, some people might say, or synchronicity. I see in it the hand of my angel.

Another incident I recall quite well took place when I was about eight. We were living in Japan at the time, where my stepfather was stationed with the military, and we were visiting a United States base about forty-five minutes from where we lived. It was during a difficult period in Japanese-American relations, and at that time there were constant demonstrations against the presence of the military. American soldiers and their families had been threatened and assaulted by certain radical elements of the population.

Somehow, during the course of our visit, I became separated from my parents. I went back to where we had parked the car, and it was gone. I think I assumed my family had left without me, and I started walking home. I had no idea how to get there, but I saw railroad tracks after a while, and I knew our home was near railroad tracks, so I followed them for hours, crying. I felt so alone, so abandoned. And, although I didn't realize it at the time, I was also in danger from the anti-military factions. In fact, the potential problem from that area was so great that the minute I was reported missing, the whole base went on red alert, with search parties, helicopters, the whole works out looking for me.

As I followed the railroad tracks, I remember a Japanese man came up to me. He didn't speak English, and the only word in Japanese I knew was the name of the town I lived in. But he put me in his truck and, without a word, took me with him all the way to our town and somehow got me to my home. He dropped me off at my front door and just drove away. I never saw him again.

My family arrived very soon thereafter and we were reunited. But I knew that the man who suddenly appeared beside the railroad tracks was my angel sent by God to rescue me. The way he appeared out of nowhere, just when I needed help most, delivered me safely, and then, his mission completed, just slipped away quietly—who else could it have been but an angel?

I thought about a great deal as I recovered my health. First and most important, I came to realize the depth of God's love for me. Although my family had always gone to church when I was young, the message had never sunk in. But now it did. I became a committed Christian, and that commitment has continued in my life ever since.

And I began to draw and paint. I had always enjoyed sketching when I was a boy, but now I began to draw and paint in earnest—and angels were among my favorite topics. I never studied art formally, but my mother is an artist and so was my grandfather, so I just grew up understanding something of art. I even thought of becoming an artist, but the places I sent my first efforts were supremely uninterested in anything I was doing. Still, I continued to sketch and to think about my purpose in life.

I was doing quite well by 1989 when I turned thirty— a good job, making great money, a healthy life-style, lots of interests. I really thanked God and the angels for helping to make it possible. But it wasn't enough. When I turned thirty it was as if my angel tapped me on the shoulder and said, "You're doing fine, Andy; now please just make a sharp right turn here on the highway of life."

I knew that what I really wanted—and needed—to do in life was to become an artist, to turn all that I was feeling inside, all the peace and strength from God, all the happiness and positive outlook that I had, into tangible forms that people could understand.

So I left my job and turned my garage into an art studio, and I began to paint. Friends told me I was crazy, that it was one of those crises people sometimes have when they turn thirty. But I knew deep in my heart that I was being called to do this—it was anything but a whim. And in an amazingly short time, I realized that I would be successful as an artist—it was what I had been called by God to do all along.

It was natural that my artistic endeavors should turn to angels. I could still see in my mind's eye the angel that had wrapped his arms around me to comfort and reassure me three years before, and I wanted, needed, to share that sense of peace and strength with others. And I wanted to give witness to the God who sends angels into our lives. I decided to paint two thousand angels by the year 2000—one angel for each year since Jesus was born. And it seemed right that the angel I painted be the one who had comforted me in my near-death experience.

As I began this effort, I knew that the angels were helping me in very strong ways. When an angel theme came to mind, I found I could sketch it out in a matter of minutes, whereas when I created a piece on some other theme it might take me hours and hours to do a preliminary sketch.

And when I began the painting, I could feel that the inspiration came from deep within my heart and soul, from the angels themselves. It's still the same today—I feel a power come out of me. It's as though I am tapping into the universe, tapping into God. I call my talent "on loan from God." I can feel my angel with his arms around me, helping to put the angels' message on canvas. We have a partnership, and our aim is to produce paintings of angels that will help people realize how wonderful God is.

People who see my paintings for the first time are often surprised. The figure of my angel is far from traditional— a mere outline of a figure with no features at all. And I never change that, because that is what I saw. It's the size of the angel, the number of figures, and the nature of the background that help produce the whole effect. I surround the angel with moving lines and shapes of paint that reflect the kinds of movement, the energy, the life force I sense in the angels. Each new painting gets closer and closer to what I feel my angel really looks like, even though the angel doesn't change, and the moving shapes become more and more refined.

What I'm trying to do is communicate something about how angels move and act in the heavenly sphere, to be a bridge for people to be able to look into heaven and sense the love and peace, to touch the angels, even if we can't see them.

When I first began my two thousand angels series, I

knew they would be helping me to translate their essence into art. And I even had an idea that they would help me reach people. But interest has grown far beyond my early understanding of where my inspired art was going. The first angel I painted in the series now hangs in the Vatican, the second is in the Riverside Art Museum; the third belongs to former President Jimmy Carter. Dozens of others are in the homes of entertainers like Lee Meriwether, Ed Asner, Stevie Wonder, Ray Charles, and Quincy Jones. And even more are hanging in hospitals and clinics, and centers for blind people.

"Blind people?" I'm sometimes asked. "Blind people can't see artwork. Doesn't that strike you as strange that so many of your angels are in such locations?"

"Well, no it doesn't," I answer, "because my angels are mostly three-dimensional paintings, and I've deliberately done them that way." When I say that through my paintings people can touch the angels, I mean it quite literally. My paint is laid on in such a thick way that anyone can actually feel the painting and trace the outlines, the textures, the brush strokes and sense the whole design, whether they are visually impaired or have normal sight. In fact, my angel paintings are often purchased just to be donated. Peter Jennings has donated one to The Lighthouse, Ed Asner to the Jules Stein Eye Institute, Lee Meriwether has given one to the Blind Children's Center, and former President Gerald Ford and Betty Ford have donated one of my paintings to the Betty Ford Clinic.

I want people to be more aware of angels. I want them to look at and touch my angels and feel the energy, the life force, the constant movement that the angels have shown me how to put into them.

Almost 90 percent of my art today is centered on the angels. It's where I should be. And I have seen how powerfully the paintings affect people, and I know it's not me who's doing it—it's the angels. People tell me they feel power, the presence of God, warmth, hope, and goodness when they see my angels, and that makes me feel so happy.

But my life is not limited to my art. Since my angel came to help me change my life, I married the most wonderful woman in the world. Her story is in this book, too. And we have the most beautiful baby girl in the world. I want her to grow up loving the angels.

Children have become very important to me. I want them to know that they can grow up in love and strength, that gangs and drugs and violence don't need to be part of their lives. I go into schools a lot and talk to the kids about staying on the positive side of life. And they write me back, and it's such a wonderful experience reading their letters.

Today, as my life continues to take on shape and focus, I know that my angels are leading me in the direction God wants me to go in. I believe that I have many angels who pass through my life, and especially my own guardian angel who watches over the others. And I pray that I'll be able to continue to move ahead and grow closer to God and help bring peace and joy into the lives of others, to wrap my arms around them all in some way as my angel did to me, and help them feel the peace and the love that comes from following on the path.

Chapter Eleven
Angels on the Cliff
Chantal Lakey, Murrieta, California

He has given his angels charge over you, to guard you in all your ways. Upon their hands they will bear you up, lest you strike your foot against a stone. —Psalm 91

hantal Lakey's experience reminds us that sometimes the words of Psalm 91 are literally true. Although our angels spend most of their time watching over our spiritual growth and development, they watch over us body and soul.

"Oh, God, help me!" I cried. "I don't want to die!"

I clung desperately to the side of the sheer cliff, my hands and feet searching for a firm purchase anywhere amidst the loose shale as slippery as black ice in the thin rain. I must not let go, or I would be dead, just like, just like . . . I didn't want to think about it; I tried to push the thought aside. But it rose up in my terrified mind's eye like a recurring nightmare, all too real.

. . . just like Dale. Somewhere, hundreds of feet below, amid the rocks and the rising ocean tide on the beach, lay the body of my fiancé, Dale. Just a second, a heartbeat ago, he had been beside me on the cliff, below me, his hand steadying my foot as he sought out a secure descent for me. And then, without a cry, he had lost his own footing on the loose shale—and he was gone. Just like that. I had craned my neck at the sound of his fall, the rocks bouncing and slithering after him. He didn't say anything; then I saw his head hit the rocks. His body went limp, and then he passed beyond my view.

"Oh, God! Oh, God!" I screamed at the top of my voice, although only the rocks and the trees above and the surf below could hear. "No!" And then, "Please, God, I don't want to die!" But I knew there was a very good chance I would.

How could this have happened? I thought. Dale and I had been visiting his cousins who lived just outside Eugene, Oregon, and were returning to San Diego, where we lived. We had both enjoyed our visit so much. It was a great place for someone like Dale, who was athletic and fit, who thrived in the out-of-doors, and who never turned down a challenge.

I settled back into the car for the long drive home as we headed down Highway 101, the coast highway. The coastward side was densely forested, with steep cliffs overhanging the coast itself. But shortly after noon, Dale, his enthusiasm for the region running high, said to me, "Look, Chantal, why don't we stop for a while? There's a trail near here I'd like you to see. I've been on it before, but no one's ever climbed to the top with me."

The trail he had mentioned was a deer trail that led

from the roadside up to a spot called Lookout Point where you could see the ocean on one side and the forest on the other. It was near Humbug Mountain, and the closest town was Ophir. Gold Beach was about fifteen miles to the south.

"That might be fun," I agreed, and he pulled the car over. Together we hiked the trail to the top, admiring the wild and rugged scenery all around.

"Why don't we take the trail down toward the water?" Dale suggested, looking at the rough path that appeared to descend the cliff. "I think we can make it. What do you say, Chantal?"

I smiled and started to follow him as he headed down the trail. Very soon, however, we realized what a foolish thing we had done. The path was not a straight line down to the ocean—it was fast becoming a sheer cliff lined with loose shale and rock. By the time we had reached a point where the path ended and the cliff proper began, it was too late to turn back. There was nowhere to go but down. As if to add to a predicament we were just realizing was serious, it began to rain, a soft, light drizzle that turned the loose rock as slippery as soap.

"How's your fear factor, Chantal?" Dale said. "Do you think you can make it?"

"Yes, I think so," I told him. "Let's try." It was hard to judge what might be ahead, but we couldn't turn back.

For a short way we went together; then, as the descent became steeper and more treacherous, Dale decided that he would go first. "You follow me," he said. He would take a few steps, testing the way, then help me as I followed him.

It was hard going, especially for Dale. Every movement

136

of mine from above dislodged a shower of dirt, shale fragments, and pebbles that hit him and bounced off his head and shoulders before falling to the beach so far below.

We were still near the top of the cliff, and the going had become even more treacherous. Dale inched his way down and his foot found a tiny ledge. "How's your fear factor now?" he asked.

I said, "Oh, I'm fine."

"Well, let me help you." He reached out his hand to guide my foot toward the ledge, and as he looked up at me, he simply fell off the ledge and to his death on the rocks below. Just like that.

I screamed and screamed. *This can't be happening*, I thought. But the nightmare of my life had just unfolded before my eyes. My fiancé, whom I had always considered to be a superb athlete with enviable coordination, had just been wrenched from my life and from my heart.

As I saw him fall I screamed in terror, clutching the loose rock desperately, and pressing myself back into the wall of the cliff. In a heartbeat, everything in my being—body, mind, and spirit—went totally numb. Suddenly, I was totally alone; I had never been so alone in all my life.

Soon—I don't know how long, really—the sounds of the falling rock faded away, and out of my shock and terror I heard only the sound of my own desperate, heaving breaths and the rain falling on the cold, bare rock all around me. Suspended between heaven and hell, in my own sudden purgatory, I had no idea what to do. Climbing up was impossible, and I had no idea how to descend the face of the cliff.

"Oh, God! Please don't let me die that way! Please help me!" I screamed again. I had no particular faith in the being that others called God—the Almighty had not played a big part in my life until that time—but I think desperation draws out of us deep feelings we never knew we had.

And as I screamed out my terror to the impassive sky and the unfeeling rock, I suddenly felt as though the gateway between heaven and earth had opened up. My words echoed and reechoed all around me, bouncing off something other than air. And I saw angels all around me like a wall of protection, buoying me up, holding me, closing in around me to keep me from falling off the cliff. I don't think I saw them as much with my eyes as with my spirit, but I knew they were there. I knew I was not alone on that cliff and I was grateful.

But gratitude cannot bring a stranded rock climber down more than four hundred feet. I clung desperately to the rock, too afraid to do anything . . .

. . . And yet . . . the next thing I remember is looking up and seeing the cliff high above me. Somehow I had managed to descend more than three hundred feet of slippery wet shale safely, and I was about seventy-five feet above the beach. I have no idea how I did it, but I am convinced that the heavenly beings who had surrounded me high on the cliff supported me in some way as I came down. I felt their presence all around me.

But when I reached that point, all of a sudden I found myself on the verge of falling, just like my fiancé. My feet lost their footing on the scree, and I began to slide helplessly down the face of the cliff, out of control, unable even to slow my descent.

"Oh, God, no, please, not now!" I pleaded. I knew that, even if I wasn't killed outright by such a fall, I would be terribly, and probably permanently, injured.

And at that moment, I felt a heavenly hand supporting me from behind, and my fall suddenly stopped dead. I stopped sliding entirely, and I was able to make my way down the rest of the cliff without incident, God knows how. I knew that the angel band that had saved me on the high cliff was still with me, bearing me up and finally leaving me safely on the beach. In retrospect, it seemed to have taken many hours, but since the sheriff's rescue team reached the cliff in late afternoon, it couldn't have taken quite that long.

I was numb with shock and terror, as I approached my fiancé's body. I knew at once that he was dead. Wandering the beach, I finally found another deer trail that led me, through briars and brambles, up the hill and toward the road, where I somehow managed to flag down a passing motorist. I don't know where the strength came from; I firmly believe that my band of angels was still supporting and helping me. I could sense their presence all around me, many, many angels, maybe hundreds of them. And that sense of their presence stayed with me for the remainder of the day and well into the night. Then my intense awareness of their presence slowly faded, as though they knew I finally understood that I was safe and could deal with the situation, as awful as it was.

The motorist who stopped took me straight into town and to the sheriff's office, where I poured out my story. At once a professional rescue team, with all the equipment and mountain-climbing gear necessary to effect a rescue, was assembled and set out to find my fiancé's body. But when they came to the edge of the cliff where he had fallen to his death, they could not go down that route. In their professional opinion, the route of descent was impossible, even with all their ropes and equipment. They had to return to town. Although I was scratched and bruised, I was not seriously injured. I spent the night with the family of the sheriff's deputy—they were angels in their own way—because there was no other place to stay. The next day a helicopter was flown in directly to the beach, and Dale's body was brought up.

"Chantal, you're a living, breathing miracle," one of the rescue-team members said to me later. "How you got down that rock face safely is beyond me. Even we couldn't do it—and we're trained to climb almost anything."

I later learned that that cliff face was considered particularly dangerous in that area, and that a number of well-prepared climbers had been killed like Dale while trying to descend.

I recovered slowly from the horrific ordeal I had been through—even now, more than a decade later, I still have bad moments. But it awakened in me the unshakable realization that God exists, and that God is not some impersonal force but a loving, caring Being. Until I found myself clinging to the cliff for dear life, I had never understood that. But as I felt myself surrounded by angels, I knew that God not only existed but had sent those protective beings to get me down safely off the face of disaster. I realized that they had always been with me to assist me and to follow me throughout life. And I learned, too, that it's foolish to waste our time worrying over all the small things in our lives that can't be changed.

What's important is our families, our friends, and loved ones, and the beauty of giving to others. We need to help others; I really believe that's the reason why we are all here. Whenever I have a bad day or it seems things aren't going the way I'd like, I remember how blessed I am to be alive, and I remind myself that my angels are still all around me.

In time I was able to resume my life, but a wiser, more aware, and I hope a more loving life than ever before. I know that Dale is with God and that he is happy. I married my soul mate, Andy Lakey—who was also touched by angels, and whose story is also in this book—and our first child was born in 1993.

Life is precious and beautiful, and I'm so grateful mine was touched by angels.

Chapter Twelve
Touching Our Angels

t's a phenomenon in the varieties of religious experience that few would have predicted a decade ago: All across the country, thousands of people are encountering their angels. Many thousands more, while not experiencing the external presence of their angels, certainly sense their presence daily in their thoughts and meditations. Even more are seriously seeking some type of closer relationship with their angels, and for many different reasons: love of God and the angels, anxiety about the future, even curiosity.

What kinds of contact do people hope to achieve? First, people want to strengthen the heart-to-heart bond that they have always had with their angels but never tried to bring into the light of consciousness. Second, they may hope to see the angels in their lives—angels who come in human form, like Robin's angel, who touch our lives, and then leave. And some hope to see their angels unveiled, radiant with the light of heaven, glorious in majesty.

Why We Seek Contact

Love of God

Our guardian angels are closer to us than anything except the love of God. They know us more intimately than our parents or our spouses. They care passionately about our spiritual well-being, and about our physical health, too, insofar as it affects the spiritual (as it always does). Since the moment we were conceived, our angels have been with us, ceaselessly in touch with our whole being. They know what we do, what we pray, what we see and say. They watch over the life and death of every single cell, and they love us, because they are beings who come from God, and God is love.

And love is the most basic and beautiful and important of all communications, as well as the most powerful. It is as simple as the child cuddled in his mother's arms, and as complex as the homeless woman with AIDS who gives her only winter coat to a stranger in even greater need than she. It is beautiful, because it creates beauty in the spirit of the one who loves and the one who is loved. It is important, because it reminds us of God, who is Love. And it is powerful, because it is more transforming to our lives than an earthquake.

Love needs to communicate. It wants to reach out to the beloved, to let the person know how they are cherished and admired and cared about. When it cannot reach out through words or deeds, it reaches out in spirit. It must communicate.

Our angels love us, and because they love us, they have only our good at heart. They want us to be happy and at peace. They want us to know wisdom and mercy and love. They want what's best for us.

We, in turn, love our angels. Perhaps we have had some sense of their work in our lives, like the hand that pulled us back as we were about to step into the path of a truck, or the wave of comfort we felt one day as we grieved for a loved friend who had recently died. Maybe we just have faith that angels exist who love us and care about us.

But whether we have seen or heard our angels or not, because we love them, we want to communicate with them. We want to see them face-to-face to thank them for their constant care and guidance. It's normal to want that kind of contact. There's nothing strange about it. Love seeks out the beloved: God seeks us out; our angels seek us out; and we seek God and all that comes from God. It's what we are made for; it's part of our nature.

The entire universe runs on the energies of love. If everything in all of our lives were motivated and powered by love, the world would be transformed. I think that deep in our hearts, we all know this, but we are afraid to live it, perhaps in hope that someone else will start the ball rolling and then we can just try to follow along. Our angels can help empower us to love, so we want to seek them out and learn.

But love, although I hope it's the hidden motive for all we do, is not the only reason why people are seeking to contact their angels. Fear is also a great motivator.

The uncertainties of life

I have always thought that the opposite of love is, in a way, fear, not hate. Hate is a nothingness, a void, the total absence of love, absolute zero on the love scale. Fear is a different entity; it's what we experience when we don't trust in the love that is in our hearts. And we do precious little trusting these days. We don't trust our children, our spouses, our jobs, our country. As a result, we can be so filled with fears, uncertainties, and anxieties that our lives are virtually paralyzed—we cannot transform them. We feel out of control, or we feel that we are being controlled by our lives, not the other way around. We want to touch our angels and feel their touch in return because we sense that they are unaffected by all of our fears—their trust in the Love whose servants they are is absolute. So for us, angels are a source of peace and tranquillity that we would dearly like to tap into and to learn from. Many people are drawn to that total serenity that governs an angel's being and seek to share it or understand it so their own lives can be blessed by it.

Of course, some people would take this too far, people who don't want to take control over their lives, but would like to be totally led by their angels. These are individuals whose ego structure is so fragile or shattered that they feel they need total guidance in everything, and would like to lean on their angels. Such people also seek contact with their angels.

Search for God

I have also found that, for some, angels are a kind of displaced God figure. Many adults find modern views of God unacceptable or too impersonal, too distant, and do not accept the Christian view that Jesus is God in human, personal, accessible form. Yet the search for God is a part of our inmost being. The need to be united with our Source is universal. It is, as Blaise Pascal the French philosopher put it, the "God-shaped vacuum in the center of every human heart." Such people often see in angels what they cannot yet see in God: personal love reaching out to touch them; ageless wisdom reaching out to enlighten them; incredible power harnessed to inspire them. (Of course no angel will willingly let us offer them more than our thanks—they know better than we that they are *not* the Source.) And I have seen that angels will try to use even this misplaced perception to lead such individuals to that Source.

Control

There are also a few individuals who will seek out angels to try to use them, control them, or bend them to their desires. Some think they can use angels for mediumistic purposes to contact the dead or give them lucky numbers for the week to come. (I strongly doubt that anyone who is reading this book is in this category.) The only angels such people will "conjure" are fallen spirits, the absolute zeros on the love scale; and it is far better to have nothing to do with them under any circumstances.

Ever and Always, Touching and Touched

The subhead here is from one of my favorite *Star Trek* episodes, "Amok Time," and has to do with the way Spock and his wife-to-be T'Pring had been spiritually joined since childhood.

I think that this is also true of our relationship with our angels. Since we were conceived, there has never been a time when our angels have left us or ceased to concentrate their attentions on us, not even for a moment. Every microsecond, every heartbeat of my life, my angel Enniss communicates with my spirit, pointing out what is good and loving and wise and true. Your guardian angel is doing the same, right now as you read this book. It's true we can't generally hear these inspiring communications, but they are made all the same. Our special angel is joined to us as long as we are on earth in an indissoluble partnership more intimate—and less well known or understood—than marriage. There is nothing anyone can ever do to rid themselves of the ceaseless care of their guardian angel. Even death itself is not a divorce, for we know from stories like those of Andy Lakey, when we leave the earthly plane, our angels are there waiting for us to escort us Home.

Face-to-Face Encounters

But knowing this doesn't stop us from still longing to be touched by our angels in ways our five senses can perceive—in fact, it probably only fans the flames of our longing. Is there anything we can do to guarantee that one day we will see our angels and be able to converse familiarly with them here on earth?

Alas, the answer is no. While we are reading more frequently than ever before stories of people who have seen an angel with their earthly eyes or heard one speak to them, such experiences are exceedingly rare. They seem to happen most often in periods of great crisis or stress, or when we need a powerful message for change or direction in our lives.

Angels are sovereign beings with free will and enormous powers and intellect, but they don't just waltz into our field of vision on a whim or because we would like them to. Angels guide their immortal lives by the law of Love, not by our desires, however noble they may be. There is nothing we can do to force them to put in an appearance, if they feel it is not in our best interests to do so. If someone should tell you of a foolproof method for contacting your angels at will and receiving some reply back, don't be tempted to try it for *any* reason. At best you will only tap into the mind of the other person, which is like the blind leading the blind; at the worst you will encounter a dark spirit masquerading as your angel. Or if someone says they can contact your angel for you, but it will cost you money, again don't be tempted. Angels have no use for money—why should they sign up with human mediums like so many starlets looking for publicity? If an angel wants to touch you in a way you can recognize, the angel will do so, and you will be in no doubt whatsoever that the being you have encountered is an angel of light. You don't need, and should not seek, a human intermediary or medium.

People ask me constantly, "How can I contact my guardian angel?" I always answer, "You already have. Not only that, but your angel has already answered." "But I haven't heard a word; I haven't seen a thing," they protest.

"Yes, you have; you just don't realize it. You need to develop your inner sight, your inner hearing first. Only then can your eyes and ears 'come around.' "

And that's the only way we can become sensitive to our angels, who speak to us constantly in tongues of angels that are far beyond human speech and hearing. We must prepare our hearts and spirits, and sometimes even our bodies if we hope to be touched in ways we can recognize as angelic. And our motives for desiring such an encounter must be pure and not motivated by any self-interest. Even then we must acknowledge that such an encounter may not come. No amount of pleading or promising will cause an angel to visit us in tangible form. Our ongoing conversations with our angels should be sought in the spiritual realm, not in the physical. If a meeting with our angel in this dimension is necessary, God and our angels will bring it about.

What Determines Contact?

There are four factors that come together to determine whether or not we will ever have knowing, face-to-face contact with our angels:

* whether it is part of God's plan
* whether we truly understand what angels are and do, as well as what they will not or cannot do
* whether our motives for wanting such an encounter are pure
* whether we are prepared for an encounter

The first factor, whether it is in the Plan, is out of our control entirely. However, I also believe that if we pray sincerely and ask for the privilege of seeing the angels of God with our human sight as well as with our insight, it may be granted.

Or course, the granting of such a request cannot help but depend on why we desire such an encounter. If our motivations are pure, and free from base motives like self-gratification, idle curiosity, or the desire to control others, or even jealousy of others who have had encounters with angels, then we may be closer to having our desire granted.

And as far as being prepared is concerned, that is a matter of personal life-style, which is discussed below.

"Cor ad Cor Loquitur"— Heart Speaks to Heart

While no one can guarantee we will actually see our angels in this dimension, I believe it is perfectly possible to have ongoing contact with them—and in fact, I believe we should all strive for such contact. We should all seek a rapport with the angels who watch over our lives.

The motto *Cor ad cor loquitur* is that of John Henry Cardinal Newman. I think it should be the motto of every serious angelwatcher, too, because it is through the heart and the spirit that we most often and most fruitfully touch our angels. They are especially attracted to those who seek the spiritual dimension of their lives.

As I have already pointed out, angels are in constant touch with us. They do not watch us from some heavenly vantage point. They are actually near us, although we cannot see them. And even when they are not sharing with us directly their own wise and true insights, they are surrounding us with their love and wholeness and holiness and light. Our different kinds of bodies may never touch, but our hearts can touch almost at will, if we work on achieving the kind of sensitivity to the presence of angels that will facilitate this.

Becoming aware of our angels' hidden presence in our

lives is not difficult or arduous, but it is subtle and requires great patience. There is no trick or spiritual sleight of hand that can tune our hearts to the angels' wavelength at will. You have to work at it.

Angelic Wavelengths

When angels touch our lives in visible form, or when they speak directly to us, even though there's no one present, they do so by coming down to our level, by changing their angelic "wavelength" to match ours so we can apprehend them. How they do this is a mystery. It doesn't appear that it causes them any inconvenience to manifest themselves to our physical senses—I've never had anyone report that their angels looked tired. But it's obvious that our senses are not discrete or subtle enough to see angels in their dimension, so they come into ours.

Our spirits, however, and our hearts, are subtle enough, so that with practice and love, we can communicate with our angels and understand their communications to us. We humans are made up of both body and spirit, and while we may live on this world in our bodies, our spirits have a life and a destiny that goes beyond what our bodies can experience. Our spirits are made for, destined for the same realm that the angels inhabit by nature. Christianity calls that realm heaven, or the reign of God. It is also called paradise or nirvana or any of a hundred other terms.

What I mean by this is that our spirits and our angels

are naturally on the same wavelength. Our angels have always touched our hearts, but we haven't understood their messages because we don't know their language. If we train our hearts to speak the language of heaven, we can touch them back.

How can we do this?

Learning The Language of The Angels

Laying the groundwork

Many years ago I decided to learn French because I planned to make a pilgrimage to Mont-Saint-Michel, the great archangel's sanctuary off the coast of Normandy. Since I was an adult and not tied to a classroom, I had the liberty to decide how I wanted to learn it. And to answer that question, I had to understand why I wanted to learn French. In my case, the reason was clear—all I wanted to do was to be able to speak it as perfectly as possible with native francophones. I wasn't interested in reading great French literature or in translating novels into English.

For that reason, I spent most of my time reading French comic books and modern plays, where all the dialogue was, and in listening to Canadian radio, rather than buying cheap editions of Voltaire and Balzac. After all, I didn't want to speak nineteenth-century French. And

I succeeded. I found that I had to listen to the Norman French very carefully and even watch their lips in order to catch the words and understand them, and it took a lot of practice to get the intonation and rhythm. Sometimes I had a headache from the sheer intensity of concentration it required. But in the end I succeeded, and my pilgrimage remains one of the highlights of my life.

If we want to learn to speak with our angels, we must do much the same thing—prioritize, decide why we want this kind of contact and what we hope to accomplish as a result.

Laying the groundwork involves taking stock of where we are in our spiritual life and trying to understand how far we have to grow. It's amazing the number of people who have never examined closely how they view the world of the spirit. You have to know where you are before you can decide where you want to be.

Exercise one: Who in the cosmos am I, God?

Knowing who you are is not an easy task to accomplish, but it's essential, I assure you, if you want to learn to touch your angels. Angels see us with much greater accuracy than we ourselves do. They remember every breath we have ever taken. We can't hope to match that, but we can and should try to recall all we can about ourselves, a kind of mental autobiography.

To prepare such a volume, you will need to set aside some quality time, when you can be totally undisturbed, and it should be at a time of day or night when your thought processes are most active, as this exercise is one of the mind and will. You should choose a quiet room or outdoor location with as few distractions as possible. Do not play any music—for this exercise, it would be a serious distraction. And choose a chair or a posture that keeps you upright and alert, not relaxed and unfocused.

Take a few minutes to get used to your surroundings and put all other concerns out of your mind. And compose a brief prayer of request for help. Mine is always addressed to Jesus, because I see him as God in human form, one who surely knew who he was more completely than any human who has ever lived. You should make your prayer to the highest Source you acknowledge outside yourself, and say something like:

> *I humbly seek to know all that I can know about myself—who I am, where I have come from, where I am going, and what I should be doing on my journey here in this world. I ask for help and enlightenment to understand what it means to be human, what it means to be me. I give thanks for the knowledge and enlightenment that I need to do this.*

After this, sit still for a minute, and then ask yourself, "Who am I?" And begin to answer, with all the detail possible, all the connections possible. There are no right or wrong answers; whatever you *are* is right. Try to state every relationship, every quality, every experience:

> *I am Eileen Elizabeth Elias Freeman. I am the girl who went to Carteret Grammar School in Bloomfield, New Jersey, and who liked to skip rope at lunchtime. I am*

the child whose grandmother taught her to read at three. I am the baby born to Alex and Helen Freeman. I am the girl who hated dusting the tabletops and doing the supper dishes, and who almost lost her cat to a killer dustball. I am the sophomore whose first date took her to the New York Public Library to study genealogy. I am the girl who wanted to become a Catholic when she was eleven. I am the teenager whose father told her she would one day become a writer. I am the woman who believes that all people have guardian angels. I am the person who would like to be less impatient when I have to wait in line for something.

These are just a few random affirmations of who I am. You can see they run the gamut.

Your affirmations of who you are should be as detailed as possible. If it's a quality that is part of your life, if it's a hope you have for your life, if it's part of your past or present, you should mention it.

When you have finished—and it may take hours or several sessions—give thanks for all you are, all you have been, and all you want to be. By that time you will probably have expressed at least a thousand statements of who you are, and you will realize just how complex you are, and into how many other lives your own light has fallen. Your angels will be helping you, because it is important to them that your self-awareness grow.

This exercise need only be done once, if you give it the time and attention it really deserves. However, any time you want to add to your appreciation and understanding of all you are, you can do it again.

Exercise two: Who are you, God?

Being able to understand the language our angels speak within our hearts depends partly upon our self-awareness. But even more, it depends upon our willingness to encounter the divine, God, the Light, the Source of both our life and that of the angels. *If we are not committed to seeking God, we will never be able to establish a fruitful relationship with our angels.* I think that is just about the most important sentence in this book insofar as we and our angels are concerned.

Angels come from God; they were created as God's servants, to reflect back God's glory and to watch over us and all within the cosmos. They come from God and dwell within the light and love of heaven. The only thing that matters to them is the fulfillment of God's plan. If we want to speak with them "where they live," we must speak to them about things that interest them.

Angels speak God's language—the language of love. If we want to converse with our angels, we must speak it, too, and we can learn to, but first we must be clear about who or what we consider God to be.

The second awareness exercise involves the same preparation as the first, but the object of our search is turned outward to God, however we conceive him, her, it to be. Once again, there are no right or wrong answers, because the object is to bring to the surface where you truly are in your relationship with the divine.

When you are ready, make your request, your prayer to the highest Source you acknowledge outside yourself, and say something like:

> *I humbly seek to understand the depth and breadth of what I know and truly believe about God. I ask for a clear vision to bring all these truths to the surface, and I give thanks for the insights that I may see.*

And then state calmly and clearly what you know and believe. If God is a person with whom you have a relationship, speak directly, for example, *I believe that you love all creation.* Otherwise, speak as you did before: *I believe that God exists. I believe that the Universe is conscious*, etc.

When you have finished, you will know more clearly than before what you truly believe about the Other. This second exercise should be done, at least in brief, before any meditation or focusing on angels, as a ground.

Touching Our Angels

Once these grounding exercises have been completed, it is necessary to acknowledge why we want to touch our angels heart-to-heart. It is essential that we understand our own motivations. Some will be high and noble, and some will be ordinary. But it's essential to establish motivation. An angel has the right to know why we want to know them more personally.

Some reasons I have heard recently are:

- I want to live a holier life in accord with the will of God, and I think my angel can help me do that.

- I want someone to guide my whole life for me and show me what to do in the smallest things, and I'm sure the angels' judgments are better than mine.
- I'm plain curious about angels, and I want to know more about what they're like.
- I want to help heal the world, and angels are healers.
- I want to contact my mother in the afterlife. I think my angel probably knows her and can give me messages.
- I want to grow and develop the gifts and talents God has given me.
- I want the angels to solve my problems for me.
- I think the angels can give me my lucky lotto number.

Of course, not all of these reasons are appropriate, and if our motives are too far afield, we will have great difficulty encountering our angels on their level. But I believe that even if our motives are not perfect, even if they're seriously off base, our angels will use our interest to draw us higher.

Seeking God

The small preliminary exercises described above are only designed to prepare us to begin the process of attuning ourselves to the wavelengths of our angels speaking in our hearts. Through them we understand better who we are, who we think God (who is the *raison d'être* for angels) is, and why we hope for closer contact with our angels.

But how does one actually establish the link by which

we understand what our angels are saying to us when they whisper their words of love and encouragement? The only way I know of is to seek God, to turn our hearts and minds and wills to the Source of all that is, and never to turn back, to recognize that we come from God and are returning to God, like all creation. That is the wavelength of the angelic heart. And to seek God, one must pray, that is, turn directly to the Divine, and meditate about godly things.

This book is neither an ascetical treatise on prayer, nor a system of meditations. There are a great number of both available, prayer techniques in Jewish, Christian, Moslem, and many other religious traditions; and as many types of meditation formats and systems as there are people to write books about them. Any technique, from any tradition, that can properly relax and discipline the physical body so that the spirit can be freed to soar with the angels is fine.

The important factor, however, is consistency. One has to work at it to touch an angelic heart. It's just not possible to dabble, although for someone new to the twin concepts of prayer and meditation it may take several tries to find a way or a program that suits one's own spirit.

Seek the Things that Are Above

In conjunction with seeking God, I believe that one must also actively seek Good in one's life. A Native

American saying, much bowdlerized, says something like, "May I never judge someone before I have walked a mile in their moccasins." If we want to speak heart-to-heart with our angels, we have to know about them and what they do. And the best way to know that is to *be* that, to "walk in their moccasins," so to speak. Of course we can't become angels. But we can become like them in how we act.

And what is the essence of angel-love? It works secretly in the life of the beloved, to help them grow in love, joy, wisdom, peace, all the qualities that shine through heaven upon us. To seek the angels means we commit ourselves not just to seeking God, but to making ourselves and our lives more godly. It means releasing jealousy, because jealousy is alien to an angel's life. It means giving up hatred and mean spiritedness, because angels are loving and generous. It means living positive lives that are not ruled by fears and anxieties, because angels know that living in God destroys fear.

And it means reaching out to others to help them. I can't emphasize this enough. If we want to get on our angels' wavelength, we have to help lift each other up. We must not only be loving, we must demonstrate our love. We must not only be at peace with ourselves, we must let that peace overflow into the lives of others.

The two national angel interest/angel collectors' clubs (see Appendix) both have what they call "secret angel" circles. The people in them are assigned a member to whom they send, anonymously, letters or small gifts of an angelic nature. It might be something as simple as a cutout from a holiday card with an inspiring message, or a note to let the recipients know that they are loved. I think that these sorts of activities are among the ways we can become more angelically attuned.

In our homes, perhaps we might do another's chores without them ever knowing about it. At work, we could send cards of appreciation or encouragement to a co-worker. Being a secret angel to someone else is an excellent way of becoming more sensitive to our angels' work behind the scenes in our lives.

Still another way of helping us become more sensitive to the presence of angels is to start looking for them in every milieu from the media to the food we eat. Angels are everywhere. The more you see, the more you will realize just how far angels have penetrated our everyday lives. In the supermarket, you have probably passed angel food cake, angel hair pasta, angel wings, candied angelica, Angela Mia tomatoes, and other products a hundred times without noticing the connection. How many people named Michael do you know? How many pizza parlors named Angelo's? How many references to angels were there in your newspaper this morning? I'll bet you can find ten. How many times are angels mentioned on the radio, on TV, in movies? There have been three TV series about angels, and at least fifty movies and TV specials. An estimated 10 percent of all pop music mentions an angel. Get looking—the more you notice, the more you will notice. And all the references will remind you that angels are so ubiquitous that we don't even notice them when they're staring at us from the produce section or a TV commercial for a liquid cold remedy (yes, there's even an angel who advertises NyQuil).

So, to sum up a short chapter that requires a lifetime to read: Angels who actually appear to us come down to our level to do so. They do this only when the One they serve deems it appropriate. As a result, there is nothing we can or should do to try to force something like that to happen in our lives. But angels always speak to our hearts, pointing out to us the loving way to live. If we know who we are, if we know what we believe about God—no matter what name we may give God—and if we understand our motives for wanting to have real heart-to-heart communication with our angels, we can work to that end and succeed. However, to commit one's self to seeking the angel within, we must also commit to seeking God and to becoming the most loving person we can be toward ourselves and toward others. And as we grow in this commitment, our own wavelength will more closely match that of our angels, who live for love and for Love, and we will be able to understand their guidance and follow it, and we will know when they intervene in our lives for our good.

Chapter Thirteen

How Do We Know We Have Been Touched by Angels?

ne of the questions I am asked most frequently is "How do you know that someone's personal encounters with angels aren't just the products of their own imaginations—or worse?" or, more personally, "I think I've been touched by an angel. Am I crazy? How do I know it was an angel?"

It's really an excellent question. Anyone who is seriously interested in the subject of angels hopes for some kind of personal contact between themselves and their angel(s). Many have had such experiences already or are seeking them. In fact, angels have become so popular these days that groups and individuals are springing up all around the country to help people contact their heavenly guardians or evaluate their experiences. Some of these are based on sound principles, some are not, and I'm sure one or two will emerge that are purely commercial and have no interest beyond money.

And because of that, the need to test the spirits, to see whether they are "of God," as Saint Paul puts it, is essential. Not everything that gives us a warm glow or a rush of endorphins is an angel. In fact, I believe that many of the experiences people have with spiritual realities are not attributable to angels, no matter how much we might want to believe it.

The reason we need to examine any spiritual encounter carefully is so that when an angel touches our lives we don't miss it. After all, angels don't come unless it's important. If an angel has really touched our lives, we want to be as aware of it as we can; we want to extract from that encounter every morsel of nourishment so that we can grow.

Although these days people are reporting a great many angelic experiences, overall, encounters with the spiritual beings we call angels are unusual enough that over the centuries people have developed spiritual helps or guidelines for examining them. The aim of spiritual discernment (or critical thinking, as its secular counterpart might be named), is to understand the origin of a paranormal experience, so we can give thanks for God's help.

Apparent angelic appearances can be attributable to any number of causes:

* A genuine angel sent either openly or in human (or other) disguise to help us.

* A deep personal longing for wholeness, for the Light, for God, that creates a vision of an angel out of that longing. (I think this is a little different from mere wishful thinking or the green-eyed monster.)
* An illness, physical or emotional, or just a strong natural emotion that produces a vision. (Remember Scrooge telling his ghost that he was nothing more than a piece of a bad potato Scrooge had eaten the night before?)
* A natural phenomenon or a human agent mistaken for an angelic encounter. (Moonlight, or a reflected sun ray can cause this.)
* A deception or trick created deliberately by another person (such as a commercial medium who uses devices to produce the appearance of an angel in order to gain money from clients).
* A deception or trick created deliberately by a fallen angel to confuse or harm us spiritually. (It's rare, but it can happen.)

All of these are possible, although in my own experience I think the first two occur most often.

As rational, sentient beings, it is essential to test any angelic encounter against what we know to be true and wise and loving and full of light. To muddy the waters of religious experience by calling any paranormal, positive event an angel without trying to evaluate the encounter, is fair neither to us nor to our angels.

Angels from Within?

If we have had a personal experience of an angel, we must examine it and the aftereffects in our lives thoroughly before we accept that we have had a supernatural encounter. It is easy to mistake our own natural and intense longing for God, who is the source of all, for a messenger from heaven.

Let me give you an example. One day I received a telephone call from a woman on the West Coast who wanted to tell me of an encounter she had had. In a dream the night before, an angel came to her in a wonderful light and warned her not to drive her car for the next three days.

"The angel was so beautiful," she exclaimed, "just like those wonderful portraits by Raphael and the old masters. And I felt so happy to see him and so pleased to be given a message. It was so real. But can an angel come in a dream?"

I told her that yes, angels can certainly come to us in dreams. The Bible—just one of many sources—contains several accounts of angels appearing to people in dreams with messages from God. Everyone knows of Jacob's dream of the angels ascending and descending the stairway to heaven. And the three angel-filled dreams of Joseph, and those of the Magi at the time of Jesus' birth also give testimony to the fact that God's angels can touch our lives in dreams. Angels will use whatever medium is most likely to attract our attention, and that certainly can and does include our dreams.

"Are you sure this was an angel and not just a dream?" I asked.

"What else could it be?" she replied. "It seemed so real. He was so beautiful and sweet, and his message must have been meant to save me from some horrible auto accident in the next three days. I mean, isn't that what our guardian angels do—save us from harm?"

Of course it wasn't my place to judge whether her dream was an encounter with an angel of God or an "angel" within. But I did urge her to consider carefully why she thought the dream was an angelic message and not a product of her own psyche. She seemed a little put out that I had suggested caution, when she was all ready to go out and lock up her car for the duration, but she promised to think about it.

I did not hear from her for some weeks, and had all but forgotten the phone call, when she called me back.

"What did you decide about your dream?" I asked with interest.

"I decided it must have been a real angelic encounter, and I didn't drive my car for the three days," she replied. "But now I'm having some second thoughts, and I still can't make up my mind about it," she said. So we had a long discussion. I asked her to tell me the dream in detail; it was simply a strong impression of the bright angel figure warning her not to drive her car for the next three days.

Anxiety or Confidence

"How did you feel when you woke up?" I asked.

"I was kind of scared," she admitted. "I couldn't get back to sleep for a long while. It made me feel uneasy."

Point of discernment 1: Angelic encounters don't leave us with feelings of anxiety and fears we can't put a name to.

Angels are beings of light; their lives are lived wholly in peace and the joy that comes from knowing they are acting totally according to their natures. They simply do not come to us, present their message, and then leave us feeling anxious, at least not without also pointing us to the solution to our anxieties. God is the ultimate Certainty, the affirmation of all goodness; inspirations from God, whether through the medium of an angel or some other way, are wholly positive and designed for our great benefit. Of course that doesn't mean that such messages are all sweetness and light. But the message, however hard it may be to take, is loving and positive and clear.

A truly angelic message leaves us confident, not anxious. No matter whether the message is a joyous one or a sobering insight, we feel an inner sense of confidence that the content is appropriate for us and that it harmonizes with what our deepest spirit knows to be right and true. Or the message may stretch our understanding of who we are and what our purpose is, because it is leading us further and deeper into our hearts; but even here, we feel confident that the message is right.

What I've said is not to be confused with the initial fear that an angelic appearance can produce. It is well known that in most cases an angel who appears in an angelic form has to begin any encouner with the phrase "Don't be afraid" or something similar. I have often thought about the notable exception—Mary the mother of Jesus. In her case alone the angel begins with a formal hello, and while the scripture records that Mary wondered at Gabriel's addressing her as "Highly Favored One," she was not afraid. (Note that Gabriel also explained why she or he used that term, just so Mary would not be left in confusion: Mary was favored by God because she had been chosen to bear his Son.)

Confusion or Clarity

"Did you understand what the message meant for you?" I continued.

"Well, I thought so. But then I was confused about whether I shouldn't drive *my* car or maybe I just shouldn't drive. So I just decided it would be better not to drive at all."

Point of discernment 2: Angels don't leave us confused.

Saint Paul, along with many philosophers, East and West, has pointed out that "God is a God of order, not of confusion." Angels come from God; and we can read in all the ancient literatures, as well as the insights that have come to the human race in more recent centuries, that angels live in a well-ordered society themselves. Is it likely that God would go to the "trouble" of sending a heavenly messenger with the capability of taking on any form and using any means of communication possible— and then leave us with a confused message?

No. Of course that does not mean God bypasses our minds. We have to think about an angelic message, act on it, and make it part of us before we can profit from it. But, as we can see from the confusion in our own society and lives, we are not yet living perfectly in the light, or there would be no disorder, no chaos. If a message is full of confused signals, then perhaps it stems from our own minds.

Orders or Invitations

"What else concerned you about the angel?" I invited.

"Well, I was worried because he ordered me point-blank not to drive for three days."

Point of discernment 3: Angels don't try to force us into anything.

When angels come with messages, the messages come from God; they're not the angels' own messages. If we receive a message that we think might be angelic in origin, and it is so peremptory that we feel constrained to obey it, or we feel we have no choice in the matter, or that some kind of divine punishment will ensue if we ignore it, then I doubt if the message is necessarily from on high. One of the most precious parts of human nature is our free will, our ability to choose the good over the evil, and the better over the merely good. The impulses that come from God, whether directly or during the ordinary course of our lives, are designed to help us consistently make good, wise, and loving choices. God has created us as beings who choose, and who take delight in making decisions; therefore, God does not force us in any way, least of all through the angels. When angels bring us messages that involve our minds and wills, they are always designed to allow us the freedom to choose. Even Gabriel, when speaking to Mary, did not say, "Mary, you are now pregnant with the Son of God. It's a done deal." Instead the message was couched in the future tense, and the messenger explained what the benefit would be to humanity if Mary chose to agree. And given a loving message delivered with clarity, Mary chose to accept the angel's words: "Let it be done just as you have said."

Message, Messenger, or Sender

"What did you remember about your dream vision?" I questioned.

"Well, I remember how beautiful the angel looked and what his message was. I couldn't take my eyes off him. I thought about him for days."

Point of discernment 4: Angelic messages point to the Sender and away from the messenger.

Have you ever wondered why it happens that angels appear most frequently in the guise of ordinary human beings rather than the heavenly, barely embodied creatures we sometimes are privileged to see? I think it's because they don't want us to focus on them any longer than necessary, but on the message they bring and the One from whom the message comes. Whenever we receive some kind of message that does not move us in some way closer to God—whether that means we pray or thank God aloud or whether we communicate our love and thanks in some less articulate fashion—then we should look to ourselves and our own creative abilities for the source of the message.

If the messenger is so opaquely between us and the message or the Sender that we see only the messenger, then the messenger is not an angel. I can't emphasize that enough. Angels never stand in the way. Angels are prisms who let the light, the message through. They are clear glass, only noticeable until the sun comes up and shines in the window. They do not want to be the focus of our attention for any longer than it takes to deliver their message or do whatever they have been sent to do.

Deeds, Not Words

"So you decided to act on the warning not to drive your car for three days," I said. "What happened?"

My caller launched herself on a whole series of events; the cabs she had taken, the rides she was or was not able to get for herself or her children, the long phone calls to her elderly mother, the rescheduling of a dentist's appointment. It had been a busy three days.

"Let me summarize," I said when she had finished.

"You spent more money than you should have on taxis, money you had to take out of the family food budget. You greatly inconvenienced a neighbor, who canceled plans of her own to take you shopping. You couldn't go to a school softball game your daughter was playing in because you forgot to ask for a ride, and one day, when your son had detention and missed the school bus, he had to wait at school for an hour until his older brother got off work and could pick him up. You couldn't visit your mother, who doesn't get out much these days and looks forward to your visits with great anticipation, because you couldn't get a ride. Your dentist couldn't fill a last-minute appointment cancellation, so she lost money because of you. And your beautician missed getting her tip this week because you forgot to ask your ride to stop at the cash machine. Do I have all this correct? Well, it seems to me that for an angelic message, a sign from God, the fruits were pretty small. What do you think?"

Point of discernment 5: You must always examine the fruits of any angelic encounter or message in your life and the lives of those around you.

Jesus put it wisely, I believe, "A good tree will always bear good fruit . . . It cannot bear bad fruit, and a bad tree cannot bear good fruit." In this case, the woman's dream led to all sorts of disappointments, confusions, and difficulties that hurt other people. The fruits were often negative, if one examined them objectively. There's nothing even to show that by not driving she saved herself from an accident.

An angelic encounter that comes from God and not our own minds always bears good fruits, tangible fruits. Of course, even when our own longing for God causes us to imagine more of an event than there really is, we can find good fruits. We're not dried up old tree trunks; we're beautiful creatures, and I'm sure all of us have produced at least a handful of delicious olives or dates so far. But if you see any real hurtful negativity—that is, bad fruits—in the aftermath of an angelic encounter, I sincerely doubt if it was angelic to begin with. (I don't mean other people's reactions, should we tell them about our experiences. I've encountered not only negativity, but outright hostility from TV audiences and even friends. But in my own life, where I encounter myself and others, the fruits have been positive.)

Message Is Medium

"What did you think about the actual message?" I asked.

"Well, it was a funny sort of thing to ask someone to do, but I didn't see anything wrong in it," she answered.

Point of discernment 6: Test anything that seems like an angelic message against what you know to be true, wise, and filled with love and light.

Another way to test the reality of an angelic encounter is to look closely at what the messenger said and did.

Angels come from God, whose words to us are always filled with light, joy, peace, wisdom, love, courage, confidence. So angels' words to us are always such as lead us to greater love, joy, and confidence. Similarly, angels' deeds lead us to light, peace, and all those good things that come from God. If the "angel" in my friend's dream had urged her to call an acquaintance to chew her out for not returning her lawn mower, then I would have assumed outright that the dream angel was just a part of her own psyche and not a heavenly messenger.

One of the most interesting points about spiritual discernment of this kind comes from an ancient Christian document called *The Didache*, or *The Teaching of the Twelve Apostles*. It's actually a work designed to help small local churches conduct their services and keep their communities organized. In the second century it was commonly expected that the Spirit would speak aloud through different members of the community who had that sensitivity; such people were called prophets. In one text the writer gives a test for discerning whether a message (New Age followers might call it a channeling) was authentic or not. If the prophet says "Bring me a meal" or "Give me money," then the spirit by which she or he speaks is seen as false. But if the spirit says that food or money should be given to those in need, then the spirit is genuine.

The principle is the same when thinking about angelic encounters. If a being in a vision orders someone to light daily candles to them or in some other way draws such attention to them that the human visionary cannot see anything but the messenger, then we must look very closely at the authenticity of such an experience. Angels don't draw any more attention to themselves than necessary.

"Feelings...Nothing More Than Feelings"

"So how did you feel when the three days were over?" I inquired.

"Well, I just went back to driving the car. Nothing special. I haven't really thought about the whole thing in a week."

Point of discernment 7: An angelic encounter leaves us changed for the better in some way, great or small.

I don't mean that our lives are necessarily transformed utterly as Andy's was or as mine was. But when God touches us through our angels, we cannot help but be changed in some subtle way. Perhaps the encounter awakens new curiosity or interest about the spiritual realm. Perhaps the encounter reminds us how blessed we are and moves us to greater gratitude and compassion for those less fortunate. Perhaps we understand better how great is our worth in the sight of heaven, how wondrous we are, what glorious creations of God. Maybe we experience a still, small voice that reassures us of God's personal love for us, as often happens when our angel actually rescues us from a dangerous situation. Whatever, there is a residue of grace, like a timed-release spiritual fertilizer, that enables us to grow. No angelic encounter is designed to leave us static, where we were. If we don't grow some or at least sense the need to grow (we do, after all, have the free will not to grow), how can we have encountered an angel?

Room for a View

"What did your family think of your dream?"

"I guess by the end of the third day they were pretty put out, what with things having to be rescheduled so much. My husband even looked up this passage about dreams in the Bible . . . "

Point of discernment 8: Angelic encounters don't have hurtful consequences for those around us.

That's not to say that we are always believed when we tell of an encounter. But we can trust that an angelic mission means us—and those we love—nothing but love and peace. Sometimes the reactions of those around us whom we love and trust can be valuable assets in helping us determine whether we were touched by an angel. During our conversation, the woman went on to say, "My older son told me I was pretty grouchy about the whole experience." I reminded her that if that was unlike her usual habits, perhaps the dream was not angelic. "If others tell you you're acting out of character, and not necessarily for the better, then think carefully whether you can trace your actions to the experience. If you can, then be cautious about attributing it to a heavenly messenger."

Freedom or Control

"Eileen, do you think I'll ever see my angel?" my friend asked. "I want to so much. Maybe if I went to one of those groups that guarantee they can contact your angel for you . . . "

Point of discernment 9: Any being you can summon at will, whether with or without accompanying rituals, is probably not an angel.

Keep in mind that angels are sovereign beings within the limits of their service to us and to the divine. They are not beings we can dominate in any way. We cannot force an angel to come to us or to speak to us, whether through our own energies, by bringing a group together to focus on an angelic message, or by using devices such as Ouija boards and tarot cards. In my experience, any being that you can compel to put in an appearance or, as happens most often, to speak out of some participant's mouth or to write things down in a trance, cannot be an angel—at least not the sort I want around. That's not to say that a group of people cannot experience an angelic presence—it happens often, when people come together in humble prayer and seeking. But it cannot be forced. Angels will make themselves known if and when *they* feel it's right to do so. And they only feel it's right when God communicates the rightness of it to them.

And when they do, even if their first words are "Don't be afraid!" the end result for us will be love, light, peace, security, wholeness, assurance, hope, joy, delight, wisdom, understanding. Probably not all at once, of course, but a promise of all we can become.

Drawing Conclusions

"So, what is your conclusion about your dream?" I asked, knowing already what she would answer.

"I guess it was just a dream," she answered wistfully.

"I think you saw your angel because you wanted to so much," I told her. "But take what good you can out of this event. It measured the real depth of your own longing to know God, for angels are just God's messengers and servants. And you learned valuable lessons in how to discern between the human spirit and the divine."

She agreed, and we concluded our conversation.

By the way, the scripture her husband quoted at her is from the biblical book of Sirach:

Empty and false are the hopes of the senseless,
   and the fool is borne aloft by dreams.
Like a man who catches at shadows or chases
   the wind, is the one who believes in dreams.
What is seen in dreams is to reality what the
   reflection of the face is to the face itself.
Can the unclean produce the clean? Can the
   liar ever speak the truth?
Divination, omens and dreams all are unreal;
   what you already expect the mind depicts.
Unless it be a vision specially sent by the Most
   High, fix not your heart on it.
For dreams have led many astray, and those
   who believed in them have perished.

Sirach's discernment here is useful. He reminds us that dreams are usually designed to tell us about ourselves and our inner dimension; as a rule they are not vehicles for visitations by heavenly angels. But we know that it does happen, so if you dream of an angel, take the time to think carefully about it. Perhaps your dream will have been "sent by the Most High."

"The Greatest of These Is Love"

Angels don't always come to us with outright messages; sometimes they simply appear and we are aware of their presence, but nothing obvious is communicated, or we only understand the message much later. In these kinds of encounters, as well as in the more traditional ones, what I have seen is that the most important criteria for discernment of spirits is Love, and especially an outgoing love. All of the other criteria that can be devised depend to some degree on this. If the angel is unloving or suggests unloving things, then it is not a messenger from God.

Love is the most basic law of the universe, the summation of all moral law, and I believe the basis of natural law itself. God is Love, and any real angelic encounter will be filled with love, because angels, since they come from God, are filled with love, too. When I saw my angel as a child, I saw that love in the compassion that filled his eyes. When Robin Diettrick spoke with the stranger she has always felt to be her angel, she was struck by the practical love that he showed in serving her and her children.

By love I do not mean romantic or emotional feelings. Love is defined by some to mean a state of being when a person not only desires the most perfect happiness for another, but desires to participate in helping to bring it about. If you have had an encounter with an angel, if your life is touched by angelic love, you come to experience greater love for yourself, as a wonderful, unique being. Out of that greater love of self, you find yourself freer to love others for the beautiful creatures they are (including angels). And you will come to love the Light, the person that is God, because God is the author of all love, the source and the ultimate object of our love.

Of course it is possible to be so wrapped up in one's self, in selfish self-love, the kind that thinks we created ourselves and are absolutely perfect, that we mistake our own dream or insight for the angelic. And if we love ourselves so inordinately, we can imagine an angel filled with love. But if that's all it is, we will notice, if we care to, that the experience has not caused us to grow in love of others or of God. Instead, we find our thoughts centered on I and me, not on you. An authentic angelic encounter may first turn us inward to deep meditation and contemplation of the great mysteries of the universe, but in the end it will turn us outward to love the world more surely.

Wonder of Wonders, Miracle of Miracles...

Miracles happen more often than we think. I don't mean necessarily miraculous cures of deadly diseases, but the small miracles that are personal to us, that serve as pointers to the fact that *Someone Loves Us*. I've always thought of miracles as reminders that the universe is not an unknowing chaos, that there is an order to all that exists, and that the different dimensions we sometimes call earth and heaven are not totally separate.

When my guardian angel, Enniss, visited me as a child, he performed a miracle by destroying the paranoid fears that had paralyzed my young life. When Chantal Lakey found herself safely at the foot of an unclimbable cliff, surely a miracle was involved. Were either of these scientifically verifiable miracles? Of course not. But, like all angelic miracles, they are a sign of God's love, whether they are dramatic or subtle.

Darker Deceptions

I never like to write about the darkness. I believe that the more we talk about it, the more power we give it, and that is a foolish thing to waste our time doing, because if we look always at the one true Light, we will be filled with that Light and the darkness will have no power over us. But it is equally true that none of us is so perfect that we can look steadily at the Light and never falter, and none of us is so wise that we can always tell the true Light from the darkness. So a word about discernment of darker spirits is necessary to round out this presentation.

Fallen angels exist, angels who, for whatever reason, do not have the best interests of the human race at heart, shall we say. Since people first wrote things down on clay tablets and parchment, the existence of these creatures has been acknowledged. They are personal beings, as angels of the Light are personal beings. And, although theologies and philosophies about them differ radically across time and space, it is important to understand that for reasons understood only by them, they sometimes make their presence known (in disguises that can be very authentic) to try to lead us astray and stop us from seeking the Light that is God. Maybe the old stories that they were jealous of us because God favored the human race over the angelic are true—I don't really know. But although it is rare, the dark angels have been known to masquerade as angels of light. For this reason many mystics who often had encounters with the angelic world—for example, John of the Cross and the modern stigmatic Italian priest Padre Pio—distrusted any encounter, whether with an angel, with another human being (such as the Virgin Mary), or even with God.

Fear of not being able to discern the Light from the darkness has prompted some to want to avoid totally any angelic encounters. In fact, the first book written in America about angels cautions its readers strongly against wishing for angelic visitations, although it acknowledges that God still sends angels to us. The book was *Angelographia*; it was written by the great Puritan scholar and president of Harvard, Increase Mather, in 1696. However, at the time it was written, the city of Boston, Massachusetts, was awash with people who were reporting encounters with their own guardian angels, including Increase Mather's own son, Cotton Mather, himself a prolific scholar, who regularly held days of prayer and fasting in order to make himself ready should his angels decide to appear to him.

Even today, many people counsel caution on the subject of angelic encounters, because of the deceptive powers of the dark. I have been to angel focus groups where the leader began by stating that only angels of light were welcome; after that the group made no attempt to examine whether the messages they received could possibly have been a deception. Merely wishing only for good angels to appear cannot guarantee it will be so. And for those who believe that they can insure the appearance of only heavenly angels by using the name of Jesus as a kind of conjuring tool, I can say categorically that it will not work. Many Christians believe that if they pray in the name of Jesus, they can drive away any fallen angels that might be near. I would point out that, according to the teachings of Jesus himself, such beings must be carefully discerned *first* before they can be rejected.

I believe that the best book on the subject of discernment of dark spirits has already been written, so I won't try to duplicate it. The book is C. S. Lewis's *The Screwtape Letters*, which is written as "advice" from a senior devil to an apprentice devil on earth, and it is available in virtually any bookstore or library. When I was just starting to learn about discernment of spirits, this slim work was my bible, so to speak, and it has not been surpassed, in my judgment.

I only want to say one more thing, to round out this chapter on discernment. Dark angels can only counterfeit the angels of the Light to a certain degree. They simply don't have it in them to enable a person to grow toward the Light, or to feel true love and joy, because they don't know what such things are any longer. They cannot produce anything but counterfeit fruits, and these break down and become bitter very quickly. Usually they don't even try to conquer our minds with evil per se. Instead they seduce us into worshipping ourselves and our gifts, as though we created ourselves and gave ourselves the abilities we have. Instead of turning us toward the one Flame that is God, they fool us into thinking that the small tongues of that Flame that light and warm our spirits are *the* Light, *the* Flame.

In any case, when we turn toward the Light, darkness turns tail and flees, and I think that is all we want to know about the subject, unless we are called to deal with it or we are fools.

Part and Parcel

Testing or discernment of spirits should be an essential part of every human life, especially if one is accustomed to seeking contact with the divine. So much can masquerade, innocently or not, as the Light. If we mistake our own spirit for the Spirit itself, then we are effectively dead-ended, worshipping our own little flame and not rising above to see the greater Light. If we mistake the darkness for the Light (and the darkness can masquerade as the Light remarkably well, unless we are discerning), we can easily become lost; we think we are heading toward the Light, but we are instead moving into a spiritual quagmire from which escape is often difficult.

If you have a personal encounter with an angelic being, or something happens to you that you attribute to angelic intervention, you must test its fruits thoroughly. Did the encounter move you to greater love or wisdom or healing? Was there joy and gratitude? Or did you feel anxiety or fear? Did you not do something you usually do, or do something unaccustomed as a result? If you felt love and joy, your visitor certainly could have been angelic, for angels leave us with joy and gratitude and greater awareness of the love of God for us. If you felt anxiety or something else negative, the so-called visitor was more likely to have been a product of your own mind and spirit than a real angel.

I can't emphasize this enough: We must *always* test any kind of spiritual encounter. To accept any vision or audition uncritically is not worthy of the children of God. We are expected to use our intelligence. It's all well and good to speak about right-brain angelic experiences, but we need the input of our left brain, too, in order to judge appropriately.

We must examine the fruits of any encounter. Keep in mind that a well can only produce the kind of water within. If a vision came from our own mind or desire, how can we grow? We can only give to ourselves the knowledge and enlightenment we already have. Angels can help us change.

Don't be afraid to test the validity of any encounter you may have had, for fear that you may come to doubt it. If your angel was from God, then you will have received a message or some other kind of help that will help you for the rest of your life. And if you conclude that the experience, however vivid, has come from the depths of your own longing for the Light, then rejoice instead at the depth and strength of that longing, for it will surely lead you closer to God.

What Do Angels Want From Us?

Nothing at all—well, not very much.

Does that kind of an answer surprise you? It did surprise me when my own angel suggested it to me some time ago. I had always assumed that my angel wanted me to show him special love, respect, admiration, and deference, to praise and thank him all the time for helping me grow toward the Light, to tell other people of all the wonderful things he has done for me. After all, I believe that angels really do intervene in our lives at times, and that they are always working behind the scenes to help us become more loving creatures.

But I don't believe angels want any of the things I mentioned, at least not in a special way. They don't want us to light candles to them or to spend a lot of time praying to them. They certainly don't want us to make offerings of flowers and fruit and other things to them, as I have learned some angel focus groups do. They don't want people to gather in a circle and spend an hour exclusively trying to communicate with any of them, to focus on them alone, as though they were ends in themselves.

They don't want to be the center of our attentions. Why? Because for an angel, only God can be the center of attention, because only God is at the Center, only God *is* the Center. The only thing they want is what God wants. Perhaps that's why people sometimes mistakenly worship angels; they don't see that they're messengers, not messages, and certainly not the Sender of those messages. The angels say to us:

> We are not the beginning and end of all things. We are creatures, just as you are. Don't get trapped into thinking we make plans for you, that we discuss your futures, that we can bring you untold wealth and perfect health and long life if you push the right buttons.
>
> We don't do any of those things, and we don't want you to ask us to do them. Those kinds of things are God's province, not ours. When we work for your benefit from our dimension, we do so because God created us to do this. When you see or hear or sense us in yours, it is because we have been sent by the One who sends us. We have no messages of our own; every single one of them comes from God. We have no personal grace to give you, no private messages of enlightenment. They come from God.
>
> Please don't be blinded by our light. Yes, it's glorious and wonderful, but it's just our nature to be that way. We find your combination of matter and mind and spirit just as glorious a manifestation of God's infinite diversity, as wonderful as you find us. Our light and yours stem from the same Source. We are created beings. We did not make ourselves. We are servants, tutors, guides. It is the way we are; we love it that way.
>
> Yes, there are many differences between our races. We have seen your world spun out of the dust of the solar system. At God's command, we helped to spin it. We have seen you grow up on this planet.

We have never died, nor will we. We do not rebel against our natures as you do, at least not anymore. We do not age or know ill health. But should you thank us for this? Should you make offerings to us? No. We are just being true to our natures. Be true to yours—grow, love, learn wisdom, unite body, soul, and mind. This is all we ask, and it is not even we who ask it; it is God who asks.

Have you ever noticed that angels never linger when they're on a mission? They don't stay to pass the time of day. They do what they are assigned to do; they do it out of love, because they are filled with Love; and they leave. I think they're concerned lest we focus too much attention on them and mistake the messenger for the message. John the Evangelist was not the only one to mistakenly offer worship to an angel and to be told, "Worship God alone!" In the early days of the Christian religion, there were those who made the same mistake. Paul, in writing to the Christians at Colossae (2:18), warned them not to be led astray through offering more to angels than is their due. It still happens today.

This doesn't mean we ignore the work our angels do in our lives. Far from it. Every day I talk to my guardian angel, and to those other angels who assist him, and I try to become more aware daily of how he helps me see the light of God. I thank him for his care, for his service to me. After all, it's only polite to offer a sincere compliment, whether to an angel or to another human being. I ask him to be a minister of grace for the day at hand, and I try to remember to thank him before I fall asleep. But I do it in the context of thanking God who has sent his angel in the first place. I find that when I spend my time focusing on the Sender, I become more sensitive to the message, whatever it is, whenever it comes, and better able to distinguish by what medium it comes, including my guardian angel. Of course I don't presume to say that I catch more than a fraction of what God is saying to me. I'm just a beginner in the dance, and I only know a step or two. But I'm working on it.

Chapter Fourteen

What Is The AngelWatch Network?

t is said that the angels communicate with each other in thought, and that they know each other's minds instantly and completely. There is no way to prove this, but philosophers and theologians and mystics have long believed it to be so.

We humans do not have nearly the same ease in communicating with each other. Nowadays we have our FAX machines and computer modems and satellite communications, but we are still light-years behind the angels of God. There are still many places in the world where the local inhabitants have never heard that the earth is round, that humans have set foot on the moon, or that cellular phones can make their lives easier. Within the same household in our own society, parents do not always know what their children are thinking about, nor do they communicate their own thoughts to their children. Walk down a street in New York City at lunchtime—you can be surrounded by people, and the only thing they will communicate to you is their intense desire not to be communicated with.

So it's hardly surprising that across the United States and beyond, all those who are interested in the subject of angels have been isolated from each other. The AngelWatch Network hopes to change all that.

AngelWatch is a clearinghouse for any and all information about angels, not just in history, religion, art, or literature, but especially what angels are doing in the world today. All over the United States and Canada, people call or write to The AngelWatch Network to report newspaper articles about angels, workshops being given about angels, art exhibits, new books, or their own personal experiences with angels. And I take all that information, add interviews, features, and resources, and feed it back to interested angelwatchers.

I started The AngelWatch Network in 1991 when I realized that there were national clubs for people who collected representations of angels, as well as mail-order businesses specializing in angels—and that very few people knew about these endeavors. I started calling anyone I could find who was associated with angel-related organizations and groups, and I discovered that the one hand had no idea what the other was doing. Angel focus groups in California didn't know that such things were also going on in Colorado, and speakers on the subject from Illinois were unaware of similar efforts in New York.

However, with the publication of the first books

chronicling people's personal experiences with angels, all of a sudden, hundreds, then thousands of men and women were coming out of nowhere to voice their interest in a subject that was almost unknown to the general public. Most of them had never shared their experiences with anyone. As a result, all those good and loving and healing experiences had been bottled up for years, even for decades, in their hearts and minds, where they couldn't benefit anyone but themselves.

It seemed to me that it would be a good and needed thing to have a forum where people could share their own experiences with angels and obtain not only more information, but further resources and knowledge about angels. In this way, people's overall awareness of angels could only grow. It seemed like a good idea. After all, there are special-interest publications for collectors of antique corkscrews, dairy goat farmers, and barbed-wire enthusiasts. Why not a national-international information organization for people interested in angels?

So I began to write up articles about angels, information sheets with further resources, announcements of angel workshops, reviews of publications, and to send them out to people who, knowing my interest in angels, would call or write. I handed them out at lectures and workshops and left them in church pews. And people began to call me to tell me of their own experiences.

By the beginning of 1992, it was clear to me that I needed to be better organized about disseminating information. I decided that the most efficient way to do that would be through a magazine, and *AngelWatch* was born. My own background in writing and in advertising helped, as did my academic background. I decided that the magazine would carry stories of people who have had personal encounters with angels, articles about angels in history, literature, art, and religion, feature stories about angels, reviews of literature and media, and—of course—the news. A good friend underwrote the cost of printing the first issue, and I started to hand out and mail leaflets about the network to anyone I could find who expressed an interest in angels. My salary from my regular job paid for setting up and maintaining the AngelWatch office. And as I got in touch with more writers, speakers, artists, and other angel workers, they put me in touch with still more, and the network expanded.

I knew from the very beginning that The AngelWatch Network was not going to be a for-profit business. I had prayed continually about how to organize it, and my guardian angel communicated that I was to provide as much information as I could without charge, and that the cost for the magazine was only to be enough to cover the three Ps of publication: printing, postage, and publicity, with a small amount extra for the usual increases in postage, paper, etc.

The AngelWatch Journal was still in its infancy when I learned that the Angels of the World, a collectors' or general angel-interest groups was going to hold its biannual reunion in Chicago that June. It seemed an ideal way to get the word out about AngelWatch and to meet others with similar interests. But plane fare to Chicago was several hundred dollars, and three nights in a hotel would also be expensive. I hesitated, even as I prayed what to do. But my angel said, "Have faith and go," so the week before the convention I stopped in at my company's in-house travel agency. It was very early in the morning. I inquired about fares to O'Hare, waiting for the bad news.

"One hundred seventeen dollars," she said.

"That's one way, right?" I asked.

"I guess so, no, wait, it's coming up round-trip," she said. "I better check this. I don't understand."

Just then her colleague dropped a FAX on her desk announcing the start of an airfare price war. "It really is round-trip," she said, surprised. "I've never seen fares like this before."

"Book it, before they change their minds," I laughed, thanking God for getting me to check. I attended the reunion, where I handed out information about AngelWatch, took in my first subscriptions, and sold angel buttons and calligraphic angel quotes to try to recoup some of the expenses. And I was largely successful.

I took AngelWatch to upstate New York in July, where Sophy Burnham was giving a weekend workshop on angels. She had graciously agreed to give *AngelWatch* an interview, and kindly allowed me to leave materials about the network for participants, of whom there were nearly one hundred.

In early September of 1992, The AngelWatch Network was fully in place and ready to reach out. But how was I to do it? The smallest ads in likely national publications cost hundreds of dollars, and, although I had put most of my savings, my tax refund, and some of my salary into The AngelWatch Network, it was not enough to pay for national publicity. Fellow angelwatchers were most kind in taking my fliers and giving them out in their stores or with their books or with purchases, and I began receiving inquiries.

Then one night, I was talking to my friend Joan Anderson, whose book, *Where Angels Walk: True Stories of Heavenly Visitors*, is deservedly one of the best sellers among angel books. She mentioned her efforts to try to interest the Associated Press wire service about a story on angels. "Why don't I write, too?" I said. "Maybe we can tip the balance down on the side of the angels."

The next day, I sent AP religion writer David Briggs a copy of *AngelWatch*, along with a letter that said basically, "Why don't you do a story on angels? They're more popular than you can imagine."

A few days later, Mr. Briggs called and we talked for more than an hour. He seemed genuinely interested in why we are hearing so much from the angels these days. Within a week he had interviewed the sources I had provided and produced a story that went out across the AP wire.

The first I knew that the story was out was a phone call from a radio station in Seattle that wanted a quote on the subject of angels for a news program. Then requests from other newspapers, radio stations, and interested individuals began to roll in. By Saturday the 19th, I was practically hoarse from being on the phone so much. The network logged in more than forty calls that weekend alone from people in a number of states and Canadian provinces who wanted to know more about the newsletter and about the other groups and authors mentioned in the article. Since that is exactly what I always hoped The AngelWatch Network would do, I was glad to provide the information callers requested.

The AP story quickly led to requests to do radio interviews and call-in shows, and more about the angels was heard from Seattle to New York. An interview I did for the Canadian Broadcasting System was heard all over Canada and the northern United States.

Angels were featured in articles in the December issues of *Redbook*, *McCall's*, and *Ladies Home Journal*. The network was featured on national television programs like *The Faith Daniels Show* and *The Jerry Springer Show*.

USA Today ran a story on angels. A second wire story on the Knight-Ridder wire actually printed the AngelWatch post office box in newspapers from Maine to California. A third wire story also went out, then a fourth, on the Religious News Service. And more than twenty-five other reporters called the AngelWatch office for their own interviews. Most of these ran near Christmas on the front page of the "Living" sections of these papers, often with color illustrations of angels.

The nationwide interest in angels peaked during the 1992 holiday season, but instead of falling back into obscurity afterward, it settled down at a much higher level. The network's angel resource list more than doubled in the first weeks of 1993, and interest from the public and the media was still evident.

Help Spread The Word

For The AngelWatch Network to continue to be successful, it needs your help. Wherever you live or visit, whatever publications you may read, whenever you see articles about angels, please think of sending a copy to Angel-

Watch. If you know of a group that meets to talk about angels, why not let the network know? If you know of an artist, a songwriter, a healer, someone whose art has been touched by angels, consider sending AngelWatch their card or address.

The fact is, even though AngelWatch now has many hundreds of subscribers, it still has no money to advertise its purpose and mission, so your contribution of articles or resources would be invaluable in getting the word out. The more information I can disseminate, the more people will begin to realize the depth of the angels' interest in us as a race and as individuals and their commitment to our growth. And the more people realize this, the more people will begin to want to work with the angels toward that end. Why, if we all become really organized in our "angelwatching," there's no telling how far the level of angel awareness on this planet might increase. With their help, we can re-create our lives, our neighborhoods, our planet.

Oh yes, if you would like to subscribe to *The AngelWatch Journal*, subscriptions are sixteen dollars annually in the United States for six bimonthly issues. In Canada and overseas, the cost is twenty dollars in U.S. funds and paid on a United States bank. Checks should be made payable to AngelWatch and sent to P.O. Box 1362, Mountainside, New Jersey, 07092. Spread the word.

Appendix
Further Resources for Dedicated AngelWatchers

RELIGIOUS GROUPS

Philangeli (Friends of the Angels)
1115 East Euclid Street
Arlington Heights, Illinois 60004
Catholic prayer organization.

Opus Sanctorum Angelorum
Marian Center
134 Golden Gate Avenue
San Francisco, California 94102
Catholic prayer organization.

First Church of the Angels
P.O. Box 4713
Carmel, California 93921

Modern-age church incorporating the healing power of angels.

NATIONAL CLUBS

Angel Collectors Club of America
16342 West Fifty-fourth Street
Golden, Colorado 80403
A large club for collectors, with local chapters, round-robins, a convention, club newsletter, and roster, dues twelve dollars.

Angels of the World
1236 South Reisner Street
Indianapolis, Indiana 46221
General-interest club, not just for collectors, smaller, with round-robins, a convention, club newsletter, dues seven dollars.

PUBLICATIONS

The AngelWatch Journal
P.O. Box 1362
Mountainside, New Jersey 07092
Bimonthly sixteen-page magazine with news about angels and their work in the world today. Sixteen dollars annual subscription in the United States, twenty dollars (in U.S. funds on a United States bank) for Canadian and overseas subscriptions.

John Ronner
Mamre Press
107 South 2nd Avenue
Murfreesboro, TN 37130

John Ronner has the largest catalog of angel books anywhere. Send a #10 SASE for his catalog.

RESOURCES FROM *TOUCHED BY ANGELS*

Caroline Sutherland
P.O. Box 70
Hansville, Washington 98340
Caroline has developed a delightful, cuddly angel doll and an accompanying positive reinforcement tape for children. For more information, please contact her directly.

Martha Powers/Angel World
P.O. Box 210425
Columbia, South Carolina 29221-0425
Martha's angel jewelry is available in many locations. For more information about where to find her pieces, please write to her.

Andy and Chantal Lakey
40485-D Murrieta Hot Springs Road, No. 335
Murrieta, California 92563
If you are interested in Andy's angel art, or would like to contact him about donating one of his paintings, please get in touch with him at the above address.

Marilynn's Angels
275 Celeste Drive
Riverside, California 92507
Marilynn has the oldest angel mail-order business in the country. For her latest catalog, please enclose one dollar to cover postage.

Eileen Elias Freeman
P.O. Box 1362
Mountainside, New Jersey 07092
The author is available for workshops and courses on a variety of subjects related to angels, prayer, and spirituality. Please write for further information.

EILEEN ELIAS FREEMAN has been thinking and writing about angels since she was five. She directs the AngelWatch™ Foundation, a nonprofit organization that searches for evidence of angelic activity, and she publishes *The AngelWatch Journal,* a bimonthly magazine. She holds a master's degree in theology from the University of Notre Dame and a B.A. in comparative religion from Barnard College. A teacher, musician, folksinger, and full-time writer and speaker about angels, she is also the author of *The Holy Week Book.*